The Tree Horoscope

Discover Your Birth-Tree and Personal Destiny

Daniela Christine Huber

EARTHDANCER

AN INNER TRADITIONS IMPRINT

Disclaimer: The author and publishers accept no liability for the healing powers and psychological aspects described in this book. Neither the author nor the publishers shall be liable for any damages that may arise from using the tips and advice set out in the book. Consult your doctor or alternative practitioner in the event of any health concerns. The methods described do not represent an alternative to therapeutic or medicinal treatment.

First edition 2021
The Tree Horoscope
Discover Your Birth-Tree and Personal Destiny
Daniela Christine Huber

This English edition © 2021 Earthdancer GmbH
English translation © 2021 JMS books LLP
Editing by JMS books LLP (www.jmseditorial.com)

Originally published in German as: *Welcher Baum bin ich? Das keltische Horoskop
   der Lebensbäume*
World © 2015, Neue Erde GmbH, Saarbruecken, Germany

Cover design: DesignIsIdentity.com
Cover Illustration: Tree circle: Daniela Christine Huber;
   Celtic wheel of the year: DesignIsIdentity.com
Typesetting and layout: DesignIsIdentity.com
Typeset in Avant Garde
All photos and illustrations by Daniela Christine Huber

Printed and bound in China by Reliance Printing Co., Ltd.

ISBN 978-1-64411-322-6 (print)
ISBN 978-1-64411- 323-3 (ebook)

Published by Earthdancer, an imprint of Inner Traditions
www.earthdancerbooks.com, www.innertraditions.com

FSC
www.fsc.org
MIX
Paper from
responsible sources
FSC® C102842

Dedication

To the Source of all life in the universe and within us, . . .

and to the realization that while there are many truths and paths, the language of our hearts is universal, is understood by every living being, and unites all with all.

Contents

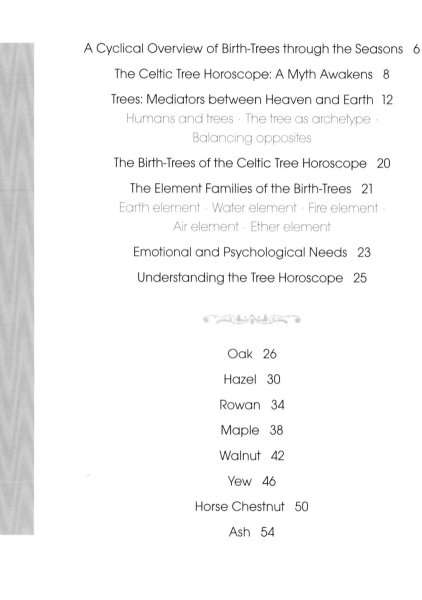

⁓

A Cyclical Overview of Birth-Trees through the Seasons

Oak	**March 21, spring equinox**
Hazel	March 22–31
Rowan	April 1–10
Maple	April 11–20
Walnut	April 21–30
Yew	May 1–14
Horse Chestnut	May 15–24
Ash	May 25–June 3
Hornbeam	June 4–13
Fig Tree	June 14–23
Birch	**June 24, summer solstice**
Apple Tree	June 25–July 4
Fir	July 5–14
Elm	July 15–25
Cypress	July 26–August 4
Poplar	August 5–13
Cedar of Lebanon	August 14–23
Pine	August 24–September 2
Willow	September 3–12
Linden Tree	September 13–22

Olive tree	**September 23, fall equinox**
Hazel	September 24–October 3
Rowan	October 4–13
Maple	October 14–23
Walnut	October 24–November 2
Yew	November 3–11
Horse Chestnut	November 12–21
Ash	November 22–December 1
Hornbeam	December 2–11
Fig Tree	December 12–21
Beech	**December 22, winter solstice**
Apple Tree	December 23–January 1
Fir	January 2–11
Elm	January 12–24
Cypress	January 25–February 3
Poplar	February 4–8
Cedar of Lebanon	February 9–18
Pine	February 19–29
Willow	March 1–10
Linden Tree	March 11–20

The Celtic Tree Horoscope: A Myth Awakens

We have finally reached the Age of Aquarius, a time long prophesied to bring great change, from transforming rigid and entrenched structures in our relationships and families right through to the way we view society. However, this change is principally and most noticeably within ourselves.

The Celtic tree horoscope has also taken root and flourished, outgrowing its mythology, but the age-old question of whether it is fact or fiction, truth or myth, is still debated. Is it just a New Age invention used to provide some amusement, or is it invested with the wisdom of our ancestors, a wisdom that leads us back to our roots, to the deepest connection with the natural world, and inner balance and harmony?

Join me now on a journey of discovery. Suddenly, we are in a forest clearing in the midst of the countryside, surrounded by trees, those gentle, wise giants. Firmly anchored in the ground just behind us stands an ancient Oak, towering up into the wide, azure sky.

We relax and lean against its mighty trunk, breathing in deeply. The fresh scent of earth, leaves, and bark fills the air. Its roots are covered with soft moss. We slowly lift our gaze to observe how light and shade play among the pale green foliage and listen to the rustle of the leaves. All our senses are alert and focused and our hearts are full, we are bathed in silence; trust fills every part of our beings.

The answers to all our questions are already here if we are ready to put our trust in our feelings and immerse ourselves with all our senses in the fullness of our emotions, as the trees speak to us in the language of our hearts. The answers will be revealed to those who are ready to listen.

We can neither find nor understand the answers to the really important questions in life with our minds, our intellect. We must learn to trust the voice and the silence of our hearts once more, and to gradually surrender to and follow their lead.

Every tree follows its own destiny, to grow and mature entirely naturally, without question or doubt. It buries its roots deep in the soil, stretching its branches toward the sun, at the same time creating a fertile environment for numerous other living creatures.

By listening to their hearts, there are those who have prepared the way to opening up the wisdom that lies dormant within us, a universal wisdom that reconnects us with Mother Nature and allows us to live a fulfilled life in inner peace and harmony. In this respect, I would like to offer heartfelt thanks to the renowned British author and poet Robert Graves[*] and the famous French journalist Paula Delsol[†]; they were the first to have the courage and confidence to write down the answers to their questions from the heart in order to share them with others in their books and articles. Their experiences, conveyed in their own words, in turn inspired others to trust and listen to their innermost voices and to follow them on their life paths. We have the sensitivity and expressive powers of these two writers to thank for sowing the seeds of the Celtic tree horoscope as we know it today.

The one certainty in our lives is constant, unstoppable change and all the associated adjustments and developments that change entails. In the same way, the Celtic tree horoscope is not

---

[*] In his book *The White Goddess*, published in 1947, Robert Graves matched Celtic Ogham runes (Old Irish alphabet characters from the 4th to 6th centuries that were etched in stone or on sheets of bronze) to a range of different Irish tree species, thus creating the first tree calendar.

[†] Paula Delsol explored the essential nature of trees in the 1970s, categorizing them in the calendar form used here.

fixed, but instead it is like a wheel of change that is always turning with its limitless creative power. If we allow this power space to breathe, it will permeate our lives and work its magic. Let us connect with what makes us strong, like the trees that sink their roots deep into the earth to find support, water, and nutrients, and stretch out their branches to the sky, rising up to the light of the sun that warms and nurtures them with its energy. Let us make use of the tree horoscope and the power of the trees that circulates within it, and become part of Nature's eternal cycle, part of creation itself.

Until I discovered this source of power for myself, I spent my life in an endless search, always looking for meaning and (within this) for fulfilment of my need for security, protection, and love. From the outside, I appeared to have the perfect life: a loving family, sympathetic friends, and financial security. Whenever I was honest with myself and admitted to feeling dissatisfied and without joy in life, I was constantly tormented by pangs of conscience: How could I expect more from life than I already had, particularly in comparison with those who had real challenges, who had to struggle to survive day after day, while things were so obviously going well for me. I felt ashamed at "having it all" and yet being unable to feel fulfilled and happy. "What are you thinking," said my inner voice, "wanting and expecting so much from life? Why do you think you are so special? Have you still not given up hoping for an easy, fulfilled life? You don't really believe you have earned that, do you?" Empty inside, alone, and lost in the universe, I felt completely out of place. It seemed impossible to fill the void I felt within. I was looking for a solution, seeking a new path, when something happened, quite unobtrusively: life opened me up to an encounter with the essence and power of trees, and they gave me the gifts of unconditional love, safety, and security. In other words, they provided everything I lacked.

Trees are always poised and ready to receive, like giant antennas or wifi networks connected to creation. If we open up and tune in to our hearts, we will be connected directly to the Source, without even having to lift a finger.

In the midst of the natural world, I rediscovered a way to access the hidden, slumbering, deeply buried roots whose network connects us all. Once we are prepared to listen to our hearts, we are immediately and much more readily aware of the answers to all our questions. Once we reach the point at which everything began, the origin within us, all our searching will reach a fruitful end. Life's meaning will be finally fulfilled, and a deep inner peace will unfold.

Creating clarity and shedding light on the contradictions that can all too easily muddy the waters of our understanding are very important missions for me. I try to use my experiences to make the power of trees tangible and comprehensible to others so that they can be touched deep within their hearts. I have written this book to share my experiences with you, to serve you on your journey through life. Rediscover your creative power, bring it out into the world, and share it with others with an open heart.

What lies behind us and what lies before us are small matters compared to what lies within us. And when we bring what is within us out into the world, miracles happen.

Henry Stanley Haskins

Trees: Mediators between Heaven and Earth

Humans and trees

Trees have served and continue to serve people in countless ways, as a source of oxygen, building material, food, and much more. The pages of this very book would not exist without them.

The natural cycle of give and take has become unbalanced as humans have placed themselves above the natural world, exploiting it without giving back in equal measure and therefore failing to maintain a balance. The Persian poet and philosopher Khalil Gibran expresses this sentiment very aptly in the following poem:

> *You often say; I would give, but only to the deserving. The trees in your orchard say not so, nor the flocks in your pasture. They give that they may live, for to withhold is to perish.*
>
> Khalil Gibran, *The Prophet*

However, the relationship between people and trees has not always been as one-sided as it is today—we have now more or less lost our close connection to the natural world and all its creatures. Therefore, let us go on a journey back to our roots, to our Celtic ancestors, and discover a bond between people and trees that is more complex and reciprocal than we may have at first thought.

The story of this bond started thousands of years ago when the Celts, an early Indo-European people, began their journey. Myths remain to this today about where they came from and exactly what prompted them to leave their homes, but the Celts succeeded in spreading across almost the whole of present-day Europe. They lived in harmony with Nature and so felt at home wherever they settled. Their reputation for courage and strength always preceded them, and other peoples they met on their travels were treated with openness, tolerance, and curiosity. The Celts shared their culture and knowledge with others and learned from them. Some Celts started families and settled down. Others continued on their travels, some heading northeast and some southwest, but all their journeying led to further encounters with other cultures.

Time as we understand it was not important to the Celts. They did not view life as a linear succession of events but instead as a constantly renewing and recurring cycle. In their understanding, to record something in writing dogmatically was to fix it in time, forming chains to the past instead of leaving people open and receptive to change in life. The cycle as they saw it would continue, renewing again and again, and however far from one another they might have traveled and however different their lives might have eventually seemed, they remained connected with each other through their roots, their link with Mother Earth. This gave them a sense of security and instilled a deep faith in life itself, from which they drew new courage and strength for their journey. They left us many small traces of their presence on their travels through the millennia. And so, just as they did in centuries past, we too celebrate the advent of a new year with a festival in which the barriers between the material and the spiritual worlds melt and merge. Following the path of this connection with Nature with our hearts will lead us to the Source, the roots within us.

The tree as archetype

Observe every tree and notice that on every tree, each leaf is a page from a book in which the Lord of Strength has chronicled Creation.

Saadî, Persian poet

Living in harmony with the laws of Nature and the universe, and with our true characters, will allow us to follow our path in life and to overcome the challenges we face with greater ease. Celtic belief was rooted directly in the natural processes and thus embedded in the higher order of things. We have increasingly lost touch with this simple and natural connection with Nature over the course of time.

Trees are poems that the Earth writes upon the sky.

Khalil Gibran, *Collected Works*

When we look at a mighty old tree from a distance and see how it stands so gracefully and powerfully, its roots, invisible to us, buried deep in the earth and its wide canopy of leaves and branches stretching up to the heavens, we are overcome with a feeling of deep trust and security. It is like being being cocooned and embedded somewhere between Heaven and Earth. Whether we see such an image of a mighty old tree physically (in the countryside, or in a photo or painting, or only in our imagination) it is not just a thing of beauty, it also immediately stimulates immense powers of self-healing and survival within us, whether we are aware of it or not.

Whether the Celtic Druids* were already aware of the healing powers of trees 3,000 years ago is not important. The key thing is that they used the power of trees for their own well-being.

The first person to scientifically prove the powerful effect of trees on people was Carl Gustav Jung[†] at the turn of the 20th century. He established that the tree is an archetype, a primordial image for people, and that it exerts a subconscious effect on us. In different cultures across the world, numerous myths have emerged and grown up around the concept of a World Tree or Tree of Life, whether Yggdrasil of the Germanic tribes, the Mayans' Yaxche Tree, Buddhism's Bodhi tree, or, last but not least, Christianity's Tree of Knowledge and Tree of Life, as described in the Bible.

The idea of the archetypal tree has flourished and has been passed down through the millennia. Its influence shapes, structures, and guides human consciousness as much now as it ever did. Making conscious use of this insight in our daily lives offers us an opportunity to strengthen and heal ourselves in a gentle way.

Trees teach us to use the power that we all possess within ourselves at every waking moment, a power that is entirely our own and not dependent on any external circumstances. Firmly rooted in the present, a tree reaches toward the light. As it dances in the wind, it teaches us to be similarly flexible while always remaining true to our nature; when challenged by the storms of life, it bends to them rather than breaking.

* The Druids were the scholars and healers of the Celtic people, similar to the Native Americans' shamans.

[†] Carl Gustav Jung was a renowned Swiss psychologist and the founder of analytical psychology.

Balancing opposites

When you can see the roots of your life as clearly as the leaves high up in a treetop.

Sergio Bambaren, *The Best Time Is Now*

We live in a world of opposites; we experience things as easy or hard, fast or slow, right or wrong. Polarity is part of our world and at the same time an integral part of our own subjective way of observing and perceiving things.

This fact alone would not present us with challenges in dealing with our daily experiences and difficulties; challenges only become problems when we make them such by weighing up opposites. Every situation that we perceive as a problem arises from a value judgment that we have made but of which we are often unaware. If we judge a situation as good, good feelings are generated. If we judge it as bad, the feelings generated are also bad.

Where do our judgments and their associated values come from? What determines whether we assess something as good or bad?

The origins of these value judgments can be found in our basic needs. We all know what we need to survive physically: air to breath, food to eat, water to drink, and sleep to rest. Our emotional and psychological survival is determined by our own personal needs of which we are often generally unaware—the things that make us feel happy and fulfilled in life, such as feeling valued, loved, and safe, and being able to express ourselves freely. These needs are often prompted by what is going on in the outside world, but it is only when we can access our true personal needs that we can identify our own authentic value system.

Discovering what is good for us, and indeed what is not, is the key to awakening our latent potential. If we live out this potential and share it with the world, we will no longer view our lives as burdensome, but instead we can feel life's joy and the myriad different experiences that it can give us. However, we must be ready to accept life's gifts as they are, in whatever guise they come. It is time to finally step back from making value judgments, to unite the opposites within us and reestablish balance at our center, our core. We will find harmony when there are no value judgments to make, when we are in contact with our own personal needs through the creative Source within us. Rooted firmly in our center, we can view opposites in a completely neutral and non-judgmental way; our evaluations of opposites cancel each other out, neither side is favored and both have equal weight. We feel no inner pressure to choose one in favor of the other. Reaching this point triggers the creative power within us and shows us the way forward.

This is neatly illustrated in the film *Avatar*, in which Mother Nature appears as a giant tree and does not take sides but instead protects the balance of life.

The structure of a tree reflects this polarity. Its roots (the soul) are at one end and at the other its canopy of leaves and branches (the mind). The two are connected in the center by the trunk (the body), through which nutrients (energies) are exchanged.

No one would think to pass judgment on the different parts of the tree, claiming that the roots are more important than the canopy or the trunk of greater value than the roots. No part could exist if it were not linked to the others, and only when all three are combined can they form a creative entity.

A tree extracts from the soil in which it is rooted all the nutrients required for healthy growth; the light from the sun that it catches with its leaves is equally vital, ensuring that the soil nutrients can be processed and used to nourish the tree. No such exchange could take place without the trunk, which connects its two extremities or poles.

As complicated as life might sometimes appear, it really is that simple: Let us open ourselves up like a tree to the exchange of nutrients (energies) between our two poles above and below, the Heaven and Earth within us. The natural cycle of our inner forces will start to flow again and we will tap into our potential once more; the key to such access lies in our personal needs.

We were aware of our basic personal needs when we were children and were able to express them naturally and easily. As we got older, we became more strongly influenced by the outside world and the needs instilled in us through our education and society. These influences and the associated needs block access to our potential as they rarely correspond to our true personal needs. As a result, what we do and what we achieve have come to be more important than our feelings and desires; our performance and achievements are now at odds with our sense of self-worth.

A lack of clear direction, a growing sense of discontentment, greater pressure at work, and the disruptions to health that result from all these are signs that we are not centered, that we have lost our inner balance.

With awareness of our power to choose freely, whenever we want, between the two poles or opposites and the happy medium, we can leave the need to make value judgements behind, return to our center, and regain our equilibrium.

Ultimately, we are all individually responsible for our own decisions, for the moment we choose to make those decisions, and of course for the consequences they bring. This is clearly expressed in the following quotation by Rumi, the renowned medieval poet and mystic:

"Out beyond ideas of right and wrong, there is a field. I'll meet you there.

Our potential, which lies dormant within us like a graceful and mighty tree, will grow new leaves."

Many moments grow on the tree of life, and each and every one of them is precious.

Jochen Mariss, author and photographer

The Birth-Trees of the Celtic Tree Horoscope

And the more I grow the way a tree grows, the more depth I achieve.

Antoine de Saint-Exupéry, *The Little Prince*

According to the Celtic tree horoscope, we can all be categorized by our personal birth-tree (determined by our date of birth). This tree will be our lifelong friend and companion and will support us with different gifts and talents. Each of the twenty-two birth-trees contains great power that we can all access in order to discover and activate our potential.

Once again, the polarity of yin and yang, male and female, active and passive is at play. Each tree species appears twice in the annual cycle, always positioned opposite itself in the tree horoscope; winter Cedar and summer Cedar people will always have the same potential within them, for example, but each will find their way to access this potential from opposite directions, from the two poles.

Exceptions to this rule are the Oak, Birch, Olive, and Beech birth-trees, to which only one day in the annual cycle is assigned. These days represent significant turning points and herald the beginning of the four seasons. The spring and fall equinoxes are represented respectively by the Oak on March 21 and the Olive tree on September 23. The summer and winter solstices are represented by the Birch on June 24 and the Beech on December 22.

Our birth-tree is the guardian of our individual potential; it will always remind us of that fact and help us to become aware of our gifts and talents. It is these abilities that we need to integrate into our lives, bringing about a whole new way of thinking and with it a change in our old habits and patterns of behavior, which hamper rather than foster our development process.

We all feel a deep longing to find the Source of all power within ourselves; the trees are always willing to share this wisdom with us, as long as we are ready to listen carefully and to have faith.

The Element Families of the Birth-Trees

Discovering your birth-tree and awakening new life forces within you.

The birth-trees share a common basis in the five elements assigned to them (Earth, Water, Fire, Air, and Ether). Trees of the same element form element families that display common personal needs and characteristics.

The birth-trees of each family and their characteristics are interrelated, complementing and balancing each other, just like the the elements in the natural world.

Earth element
Imaginative and practical, connoisseurs and esthetes
The Earth element family includes the Walnut, Horse chestnut, Olive, Apple, and Fig trees. They share the characteristics below:

A strong need for security and intimacy; a focus on taking action and serving others; efficiency; a concentration on security; a family focus; manual dexterity and creativity; close links to the soil; sensuous esthetes; good at organizing and managing (administration); very tolerant.

Water element
Empathetic teachers and creative people

The Water element family includes the Birch, Fir, Elm, Willow, and Linden trees. They share the following characteristics:

A strong need to express their feelings and vitality; emotional ups and downs; a family focus; a strong sense of justice; a caring and sympathetic nature; great vitality; very flexible and adaptable; a strong intellect; a desire to pass on experience to others.

Fire element
Adapable and enthusiastic, spirited motivators

The Fire element family includes the Oak, Hazel, Rowan, Hornbeam, and Pine trees. They share the following characteristics:

A strong impulse for change and enjoyment of life; a focus on essentials; pioneers in many fields; a drive for dominance; like to express themselves by communicating with others; a driving force; interested in life and open-minded; adaptable through a willingness to change.

Air element
Dynamic dreamers and inventors

The Air element family includes the Beech, Cypress, Maple, and Ash trees. They share the following characteristics:

A strong need for freedom and clarity; explorers with a love of travel; a wide variety of interests; a reliance on the head rather than the heart; open to new experiences and encounters; like to communicate with others; an inquisitive nature; a refreshing spontaneity; ambitious; place great value on individuality and independence.

Ether element
Intuitive visionaries and networkers

The Ether element family includes the Poplar, Cedar, and Yew trees. They share the following characteristics:

A strong need for love and transcendence; a natural leader; a patient and persistent focus on moving forward in life; tolerant and open-minded; sensitive perception; a compassionate nature as well as Nature-loving; searching for insight; a desire for horizon-broadening and inspiring travel; an articulate networker.

What is Ether?
It was the Greek philosopher Aristotle (born 384 BCE), a pupil of Plato, who devised the term Ether to describe the fifth element. Its Latin name *quinta essentia* translates as the "fifth essence." Aristotle teaches that the four elements of Earth, Water, Fire, and Air all originate from Ether, which has the power to breathe life into all things and to interweave the visible with the invisible. Ether is the space that connects everything. Each of these five elements has its own special qualities and roles. If just one element were to be absent, our planet Earth would not exist as we know it. The birth-trees of the Ether family elements have a particular challenge: to make a connection between the invisible and visible worlds. Bringing this gift into the material world requires humility and trust in creation.

Emotional and Psychological Needs

Our soul longs for experience and urges us to satisfy this inner hunger by fulfilling our basic emotional and psychological needs. To help us achieve this, it sends us impulses or prompts in the form of thoughts and ideas, and stimulates our emotions and feelings. Since we live in a dual world, our mind inevitably categorizes these prompts as good or bad, but in fact these basic needs are neutral, and simply require us to acknowledge and pay attention to them in order to try and satisfy them in some way.

As previously mentioned, each tree sign is assigned to an element family and each element family has certain strong, basic emotional and psychological needs that are specific to that family (p. 21).

If we are not able to satisfy these needs, we feel out of balance and disturbed, ill at ease. The result may be that our thoughts go around in circles and our emotions erupt, or we could simply become overwhelmed by our feelings.

It is then time to look within us to discover which of our emotional and psychological needs want to be heard. The element family of our tree sign helps us to recognize which are our most powerful needs in this life.

Once we are ready to address the process of personal development and to move on in life, our deepest desires will be met. We should approach this with emotional honesty and awareness, while patience, perseverance, and a sense of humor can also be a great help along the way.

Let go of the idea that your needs will be met in some specific manner. Instead, allow life to fulfill you in its own way. Have confidence: everything that happens in your life serves your best interests.

Every true desire within a person is a hidden wing to take them home.

Otto von Loeben, German author

Understanding the Tree Horoscope

Before you read your first horoscope, the following explanations of the headings used in this book may be helpful.

Carpe arborem

Loosely translated, carpe arborem means "use the wisdom of the tree."

This paragraph describes the fundamental philosophy of a person with the birth-tree featured and provides insights into the tree energy that is active on the days listed. This energy can be used by everyone with that birth-tree to help them shape their lives more consciously.

In a nutshell

This is a concise summary of what people should pay attention to, should they wish to gently restore flow in their lives. We can be sure of one thing: Change always begins with ourselves, whether we are aware of it or not. We have a choice, we can either take matters into our own hands or wait until life confronts us with change, suddenly and abruptly.

Healing powers

Given the wide range of applications and healing powers derived from the different parts of each birth-tree, only a few healing powers are able to be included under this heading.

Inspiration

An inspirational quote by a famous person who shares the relevant birth-tree.

Oak

Element family: Fire

Gifts and talents

Spirited, strong-willed, full of joie de vivre and a thirst for action; optimistic, with a sense of responsibility; a born leader, with a zest for adventure; obstinate, persistent.

Carpe arborem

The strength to find myself and to express my individuality is to be found only and exclusively in the here and now, in humility toward creation.

Symbolism

The Oak is associated with just one day in the year and represents the spring equinox. This is a time of balance, when day and night are of equal length. This day should be used for reviewing the winter months that have just passed, looking for insights that will assist us in gratefully letting go of the past in order to make way for the new. For the Celts the Oak was a symbol of steadfastness, resilient strength, and power. Centuries ago, the Druids were already aware of the extraordinary healing powers of Oak mistletoe, which is now used in the treatment of cancer.

The Oak path through life

Oak-born people belong to the family of Fire elements, the source of the clarity, speed, and strength with which they are able to progress in life, be fulfilled, and achieve their goals. They are at the center of the action and have a gift for attracting and holding the attention of the people around them. They pay no heed to setbacks, but instead draw fresh strength from them,

The pulsating, vital power of the moment

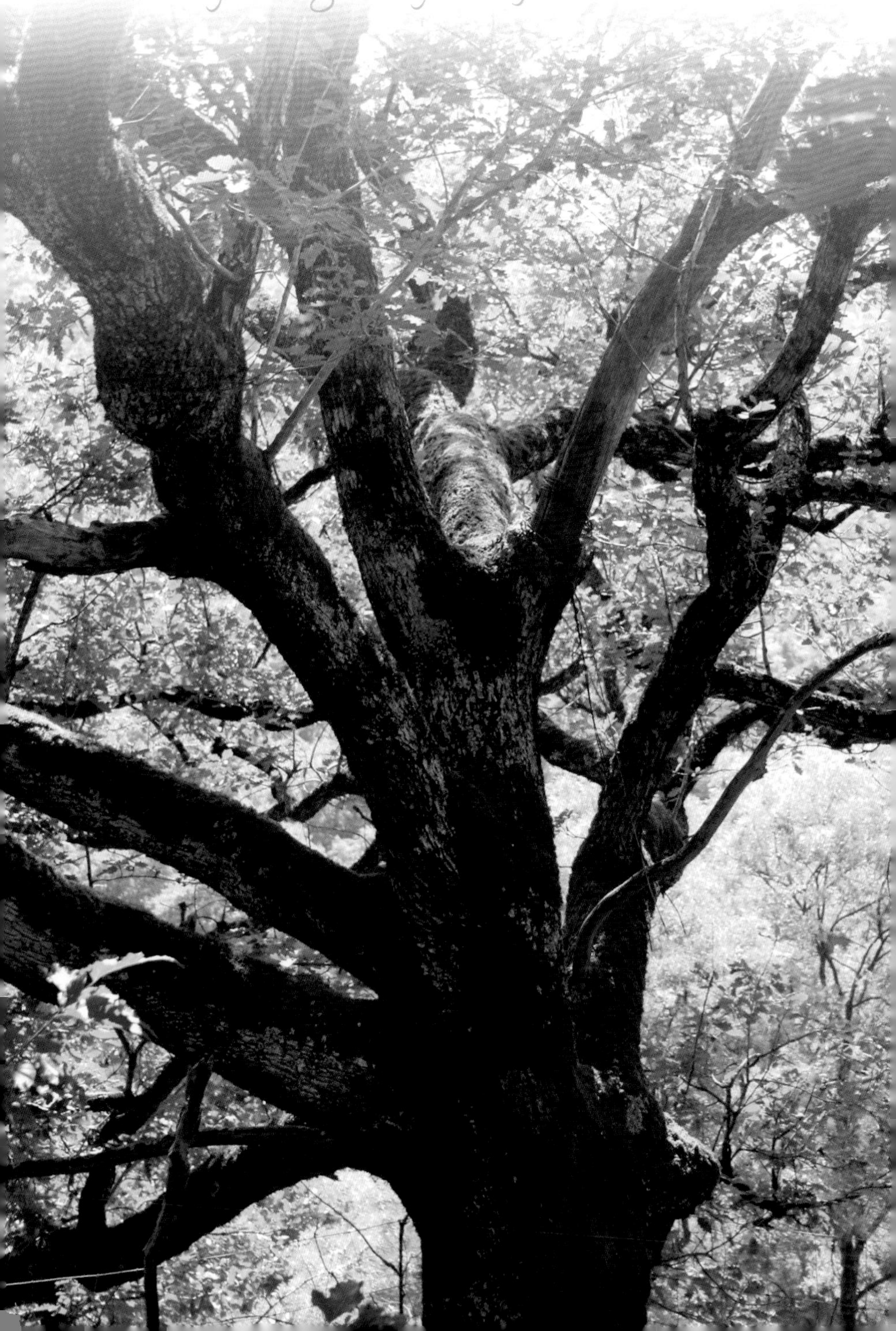

viewing them as an incentive to power their way forward. Their focus is always on their goal, and once they have decided upon something, any attempt to distract them is futile and only leads to frustration. The famous quote *Veni, vidi, vici* ("I came, I saw, I conquered") by the Roman general Julius Caesar neatly sums up the character of an Oak personality in just a few words.

Strong-willed and spirited, these born leaders do not simply walk into a room, but instead make an entrance, knowing exactly what they want and how to get it. They have an ability to focus all their attention on the most important and decisive thing in life, namely on this single present moment. This allows these positive people to achieve almost anything with an effortless, almost whimsical ease, while others spend their entire lives striving to achieve such a wise and powerful attitude to life. However, as the proverb says, pride can come before a fall, and Oak-born people have to learn that competitive behavior and vanity may do them no favors and could even prevent them from achieving their objectives. They should make sure that they deal with their fellow human beings with respect and dignity in both private and professional circumstances. The mark of a born leader is a healthy understanding of the idiosyncrasies of others, coupled with a sympathetic ear and compassion for their problems and concerns.

All professional doors are open to Oak-born people, except those that lead to unskilled work carried out alone, such as in an office, in situations where proactive or independent thought are not required. They cannot develop their great potential as natural leaders in the shadow of others. They want to (and ideed should) bask and glow in the light of the sun.

In a nutshell

The gift enjoyed by these born leaders of being able to attract the attention of many brings with it the responsibility of not making self-serving decisions, but instead making choices that benefit everyone. Most Oak-born people are only too aware of their own talents; they have a tendency to develop strong egos and to neglect the needs of their fellow humans. They should learn that for a leader it is not the size of their ego that matters, but the size of their heart, and their ability to empathize with others. Admitting mistakes and weaknesses and relinquishing any decisions to which they have been stubbornly clinging are signs of strength. Their pride may be hurt, but they will reach their goals more quickly and with greater certainty.

Healing powers
A tea made from the bark or leaves of the Oak has anti-inflammatory, astringent, and antiseptic properties.

Birth-tree power
The pulsating, vital power of the moment.

Inspiration from an Oak personality

The day it arrives, it will arrive. It could be today or 50 years later. The only sure thing is that it will arrive.

Ayrton Senna
Brazilian Formula 1 racing driver
(after a fellow driver's fatal accident)

Hazel

March 22–31 and September 24–October 3

Element family: Fire

Gifts and talents

Honest, wise, and open to new things; reliable, pugnacious, successful, talented in many areas; generous, magnanimous, tough, and tolerant; a love of travel; a magnetic personality; sensuous, assertive.

Carpe arborem

I perceive with my heart the truth that is hidden from my senses.

Symbolism

In Celtic mythology, Hazel is a symbol of wisdom, truth, and fertility. The Druids would make divining rods from its branches and use them to locate water underground. Today, as then, water remains crucial for survival. In Ancient Rome, Hazel was a symbol of peace.

The Hazel path through life

Hazel-born people belong to the family of Fire elements, which gives them their assertive temperament and transformative power in all their relationships. They set themselves the goal of seeking new challenges and succeeding in new spheres of life; they are generally also very successful in both their professional and private lives. Their character is also reflected in their desire to explore distant countries, so Hazel personalities are often tempted to travel the world, even at an early age. They have adventurous souls and are frequently the rebel of their family from a young age. Hazel-born people will face up to any confrontation with courage in their desire to shake up the status quo

The potent power of groundbreaking pioneers

and overcome inflexibility. In so doing, they learn how to grow beyond their own limitations and discover new paths in life.

Hazel personalities like to assert themselves and to be noticed and successful; they do not shy away from confrontation. They stand up for their own truth, while their intuition tells them instantly if someone else is not being similarly honest. In emotionally charged arguments, they should be careful to react sympathetically and to choose their words and actions with care, rather than give full rein to their often stubborn natures with what can sometimes be rather hurtful comments. Thanks to their ability to accept without question those things they cannot change, and yet at the same time with the strong will and assertiveness that allows them to change what is within their power, they will clear the way for the next generation. All that life demands of them in return is to have sufficient patience to achieve this.

In their choice of career, Hazel-born people are often trend-setters, way ahead of their time, hence they are very interested in new areas of research and roles in professions such as osteopathy, working with animals in non-orthodox ways (such as horse-whispering), and spiritual mediation. At the same time, they have a sound idea of what professions will be needed in the future and are at the front of the queue when it comes to trailblazing the way forward in a new sphere.

In a nutshell

To think before they speak is advice that Hazel personalities would do well to take on board. They have a tendency to be overly hasty and unrestrained when dishing out truths to others. Even if they are right in what they say, such behavior will not bring about the change they hope for in the other person. Instead, this aggressive approach generally elicits resistance and the metaphorical bringing down of shutters, with the result that the key elements of any potentially helpful message are therefore neither received nor taken on board. Trailblazers are expected not simply to preach how things might be done better, but also to follow up such wisdom with action.

Healing powers
The leaves and bark of the Hazel tree have hemostatic (blood-staunching) and antipyretic (fever-lowering) properties. Hazelnuts are rich in vitamins A, B, and C, valuable minerals, and essential fatty acids, making them useful in treatments for both skin and nerves.

Birth-tree power
The potent power of groundbreaking pioneers.

Inspiration from Hazel personalities

The paths are many, but the goal is one.

Rumi
medieval Persian mystic and poet

We must be the change we wish to see in the world.

Mahatma ("Great Soul") Gandhi
Indian lawyer, and political and spiritual leader
of the Indian independence movement

Rowan

April 1–10 and October 4–13

Element family: Fire

Gifts and talents

Helpful, enthusiastic, visionary; bursting with joie de vivre; generous, wise, with an eye for beauty; open to new things, sociable, with a sense of justice; a seeker of inner balance; a good listener and organizer.

Carpe arborem

Exploring myself and finding within me the things that bring me joy creates balance, gives me strength, and awakens my love for myself.

Symbolism

Thanks to its red berries, the Rowan, sometimes known as the Mountain Ash, is a popular source of food for many animals, especially birds. It is also considered a wise herald of emerging change. Through its humility and wonderful adaptability to its environment, it is a symbol for pure joy in life.

The Rowan path through life

Rowan-born people belong to the Fire elements family, which is the source of their spirited nature and constant focus on the essentials. They radiate grace, beauty, and inner serenity, which is why many people feel safe and accepted around them. These enthusiastic travelers always find new things and places to experience and explore, and their great thirst for adventure draws them out into the world. With this often comes the restlessness of youth that grants little peace.

The balancing power of self-love

Rowan personalities are sympathetic listeners and mediators between opposites. Their intuitive wisdom allows them to help their fellow humans find inner equilibrium, thereby restoring harmony to potentially unbalanced relationships. They similarly feel a deep yearning for agreement and harmony themselves.

However, what they find easy to deal with around others presents one of their own greatest challenges in life; if the demands and expectations that others have of them are not in tune with their own personal needs, Rowan personalities all too readily place their own needs at the back of the queue. This selfless character trait might seem agreeable to others at first sight, but it does not help either party when viewed over the longer term.

This pattern of behavior can result in those with Rowan as their birth-tree becoming unbalanced and emotionally distanced from others. A further consequence is the manifestation of long-standing pent-up anger, which then hinders the communication of feelings and naturally makes finding a solution all the more difficult and protracted. It is hugely important for them to listen to and follow their inner voice in order to find within themselves the stability they seek in the outside world. Mastering life for them lies in first giving themselves what they so keenly seek in others: support, a sense of security, and love. This will give them the courage to follow their dreams.

Rowan-born people also long to express their sense of harmony in their professional lives. Combined with an appreciation of beauty and creativity, this makes them suitable in particular for professions with lots of social involvement and for roles as designers, interior decorators, and stylists. A desire for authority means that their professional path often leads to self-employment or working with a business partner on an equal footing.

In a nutshell

It is important for the self-worth of Rowan-born people to ensure that the expectations and wishes of others do not overpower them. They should first be clear about their own needs in order to be able to stand up for these both openly and honestly. This clarity, combined with expressing their needs to others, will bring them the level of stability, trust, and inner balance that they need to progress along their life path step-by-step.

The lesson they should learn is to open their heart to every experience, whether joyful or painful, instead of hiding behind supposedly protective walls. Those with Rowan as their birth-tree should learn to stop making decisions with their precocious intellects and instead look within themselves and leave the choice to their hearts.

Healing powers

Rowan berries can be eaten in small quantities, whether raw, cooked, or dried. They contain large amounts of vitamin C, boost the immune system, and cleanse the blood. They also stimulate kidney function.

Birth-tree power

The balancing power of self-love.

Inspiration from a Rowan personality

I saw that you must often begin with a deception in order to reach the truth; light must necessarily be preceded by darkness.

Giacomo Casanova
Italian adventurer and author

Maple

Element family: Air

Gifts and talents

Loves freedom, ambitious, strong-willed, sociable; very active, decisive, courageous, and eager to move forward; multitalented, socially involved, confident.

Carpe arborem

Discovering who I am and expressing my feelings leads me to a freedom beyond all boundaries that dwells in my heart.

Symbolism

Maple trees are also commonly known as "angel-head trees," as their winged fruits could be said to resemble dancing angels, spinning around rapidly as they fall from the treetop to the ground. Maples can be found almost throughout the world and their leaves, shaped like the palm of an outstretched hand, have become a symbol of freedom.

The Maple path through life

Maple-born people belong to the family of Air elements, the source of their great spontaneity, openness, and eloquence. They are seekers, propelled by an inner drive and desire to discover and define themselves and their true identity. As an Air element personality, they feel at home everywhere and yet nowhere.

People with this birth-tree test the limits of their many and diverse talents on their very individual journeys through life. They face a constant succession of new challenges, but as long as they learn to trust their intuition, they succeed in overcoming them easily and often in an unconventional way. Maple-born

The liberating power of identity

people start out as courageous lone warriors, even from an early age, soon freeing themselves from generally well-protected and strict family structures. Thanks to their exceptionally sociable and helpful natures, they gravitate more toward groups as they accumulate life experiences.

Maple personalities have a positive and visionary attitude to life, the driving force behind their ability to forge ahead with their wealth of ideas, which they are happy to share with like-minded people. They also aspire to encourage and support their fellow human beings in their ongoing personal development. This is echoed in the selection of the Maple as a rallying symbol for the French Revolution, with its motto of "Liberty, Equality, Fraternity." Maple-born people have an Achilles heel, however, in the form of frequently long-held, pent-up anger, to which they may give vent unexpectedly. One way for them to avoid this is to use their creativity in all aspects of their lives, since anger is merely suppressed creativity.

The trunk of a Maple tree often starts to fork low down, just as Maple personalities can be deeply split and harbor an inner contradiction. Their heartfelt longing for togetherness or intimacy is generally overshadowed and blocked by the fear that it might result in a loss of freedom and ultimate surrender. This inner conflict strives constantly for balance and can lead to moodiness and unease. Their ultimate success will be to recognize that love and freedom (perceived as being at odds with each other by many people) are in reality dependent on each other and unable to exist without one another.

Their social commitment is also reflected in their choice of profession. The speed at which they live their lives makes it difficult for many of their peers to keep up with them, so Maple-born people should learn to be considerate of others. The focus in their professional lives is often on collaborating and working with others. With their exceptional intellects and wide variety of interests, they are also suited to becoming researchers, academics, and philosophers.

In a nutshell
The key factor for Maple-born people is to recognize that they have the freedom to choose and are not held prisoner by past decisions. One of the lessons they must learn is to find the freedom they seek in the outside world within themselves; it is inner change that leads to inner freedom. They will slowly learn to open up their hearts to those closest to them and to trust again. It is never too late to make another, different choice as long we are ready to express our feelings to others honestly and open ourselves up to a life of togetherness.

Healing powers
The leaves, bark, and syrup of the Maple have cooling, decongestant properties and are used to treat fever, inflammation of the eyes, and insect bites. Maple syrup, the highly prized sweet sap of the sugar Maple, has calming properties and can soothe aggression.

Birth-tree power
The liberating power of identity.

Inspiration from a Maple personality

Failure is unimportant. It takes courage to make a fool of yourself.

Charlie Chaplin
British comic actor and filmmaker

Walnut

April 21–30 and October 24–November 2

Element family: Earth

Gifts and talents

Family-oriented, creative, persistent, loyal; values security; a connoisseur; strong-willed, capable, obstinate, gentle; a seeker of harmony and emotional stability; appreciative of art and culture.

Carpe arborem

Nature and expressing my creativity bring my restless spirit inner peace and help me to rediscover and experience a sense of security in my heart.

Symbolism

In Ancient Greece, the fruit of the Walnut was a food for the gods and a symbol of good luck and fertility. In Celtic mythology, the Walnut tree symbolized the departure for fresh fields and pastures new, and all the changes that this entails.

The Walnut path through life

Walnut-born people belong to the family of Earth elements, which allows them to give concrete shape to their ideas and thinking without losing their intellectual footing. In the professional world, they are most likely to find themelves working as researchers and technicians. They are also eloquent speakers. Wherever they go they bring with them a clean slate, sweeping away old habits in favor of new ideas and ways of thinking.

Walnut-born people are the great thinkers among those who like to present a hard, protective shell to the world to equip them for what is generally a rebellious and pioneering path in life.

They are often seen as the infamous black sheep of the family, or as challenging mavericks at school, while in the workplace they gain a reputation as lateral thinkers who sometimes disrupt and "set the cat among the pigeons." Walnut personalities set themselves the goal of making a clean sweep of things: discarding old habits and long outmoded traditions, along with outdated beliefs and fossilized structures, while highlighting and dealing with grievances and clearing space for the new. These loyal and sensitive people derive their strength and energy from their secure relationships within their own families, which they are usually aware of from a very early age.

Their restless minds generally hop from one thought to the next, generating an inner drive that can reveal itself in the form of stress and a consistently tense attitude. However, by spending time in the natural world and using their creativity, they can relax a little and quieten their minds, which are otherwise always buzzing with thoughts and ideas, and in so doing find some inner peace and calm.

In a nutshell
One of Walnut-born people's greatest challenges is to find some calm and stillness by silencing their restless thoughts. It is when they are surrounded by peace and quiet that they can get back in touch with their feelings. Failure to do so can manifest itself physically in the form of severe headaches or eye problems. Like all Earth element personalities, Walnut-born people find it difficult to let go of the structures they build around them that provide security and stability. However, letting go is a skill they must learn or even the slightest change can provoke a total emotional collapse.

Healing powers
Walnut leaf tea has astringent and anti-inflammatory properties and can be used for digestive complaints.

Birth-tree power

The emotional power of a sense of security.

Inspiration from a Walnut personality

For believers, God is in the beginning, and for physicists, He is at the end of all considerations.

Max Planck
German physicist and Nobel Prize laureate

Yew

May 1–14 and November 3–11

Element family: Ether

Gifts and talents

In touch with Nature; contrary; a mystical aura; highly sensitive, loving, sensuous, gentle; a vivid imagination; spiritual and mental depth; artistic talent.

Carpe arborem

I unite the seeming opposites in life within me, such as joy and suffering, birth and death. I sense the eternity of being and a connection with the infinite universe in every moment.

Symbolism

As the tree of death and eternal life, for the Celts the Yew symbolized the link between this world and the next, between birth and death.

Given this symbolism, and many of its characteristics, including its evergreen needles, toxicity, and the hallucinogenic properties of the vapors it gives off, it can be assumed that Yggdrasil, the mythical tree that supports the universe, is not an Ash but a Yew tree.

The Yew path through life

Yew-born people belong to the family of Ether elements, which gives them their sensitive, and indeed often extrasensory, perception of the world. This explains why they find it easy to call on the more creative and imaginative sides of their nature and why their talents are best put to use in artistic fields or in designing natural environments. They also often act as a barometer for the future, with a vision for new ways of shaping society into something more open-minded and compassionate.

The creative power of sensitivity

Yew-born people are frequently completely unaware of this special gift that is waiting to be unleashed upon the world. If they fail to make the leap that will channel their great sensitivity into creative areas, their mood may become low and they may even sink into depression, hiding their vulnerability behind a mask of cynicism, or even develop aggressive defense mechanisms.

Revered by the Celtic people as the tree of death, the Yew (and Yew-born people) are tasked with watching over the consciousness of the immortality of the soul and the eternal circle of life. People with this birth-tree attach great importance to turning their vocation into their profession. Anything is possible: from musician, poet, or teacher of hypersensitive children to becoming a spiritual companion and end-of-life carer. Sooner or later, Yew-born people have to find a way of channeling their sensitive gift and find new ways for using it. This will help to stabilize their emotions and allow them to find a foothold in the material world.

They also serve their fellow human beings, who long for their deep compassion and warmth, especially when life events or crises drive these people to the edge of the abyss. Yew personalities are often deeply affected by their personal experiences with death during their lives. This enables them to act as a link between this world and the next by passing on what they have learned to those who have had to say farewell to loved ones and are in need of compassionate support in the process of letting go.

In a nutshell

The more sensitive and delicate the person within, the tougher and cooler the facade can appear, which is often the case with Yew-born people. To escape life's harsh reality, they may take refuge behind protective walls of cynicism and sarcasm, cigarettes, alcohol, and other addictive substances. They should learn that this is ultimately pointless and brings only temporary relief. Being in the natural world and being able to make use of their creativity will help guide them back to emotional balance and inner stability.

Healing powers
Apart from the red outer covering of the seed cone, every part of the Yew is toxic. Following the well-known adage attributed to the 16th-century Swiss physician Paracelsus that "the dose makes the poison," it is used as a trace element in tonics for the heart and cancer-inhibiting substances.

Birth-tree power
The creative power of sensitivity.

Inspiration from a Yew personality

It is important to make a dream of life and of a dream reality.

Nothing in life is to be feared, it is only to be understood.

Life is not easy for any of us. But what of that? We must have perseverance and above all confidence in ourselves. We must believe that we are gifted for something and that this thing, at whatever cost, must be attained.

Marie Curie
Polish chemist, physicist, and Nobel laureate

Horse Chestnut

May 15–24 and November 12–21

Element family: Earth

Gifts and talents

Open, courageous, spontaneous, enthusiastic, adventurous, and honest; self-critical, consistent, adaptable, patient, and straightforward; helpful, attentive, vigorous, with a strong sense of justice; thrifty, reliable.

Carpe arborem

Opening myself up sympathetically to my inner being gives me confidence and the strength to leave old habits behind me in order to find my true goals on new life paths.

Symbolism

The Horse chestnut is a symbol of conscientiousness and openness to one's environment.

The Horse chestnut path through life

Horse chestnut-born people belong to the family of Earth elements, the source of their helpful and responsible natures. Just like the fruit of the Horse chestnut, people with this birth-tree conceal a soft and sensitive core within the spiky and hard shell that they present to the outside world. Horse chestnut personalities are among the most disciplined, ambitious, and grounded in the tree horoscope. They fulfill themselves by usefully contributing to a community with which they personally identify, so they can be of help for the good of everyone. They will therefore use their talents effectively in a career where they can be involved with a community or society in general, where they can make a contribution, both within a wider group of like-minded people, such as the

The authentic power of pure humor

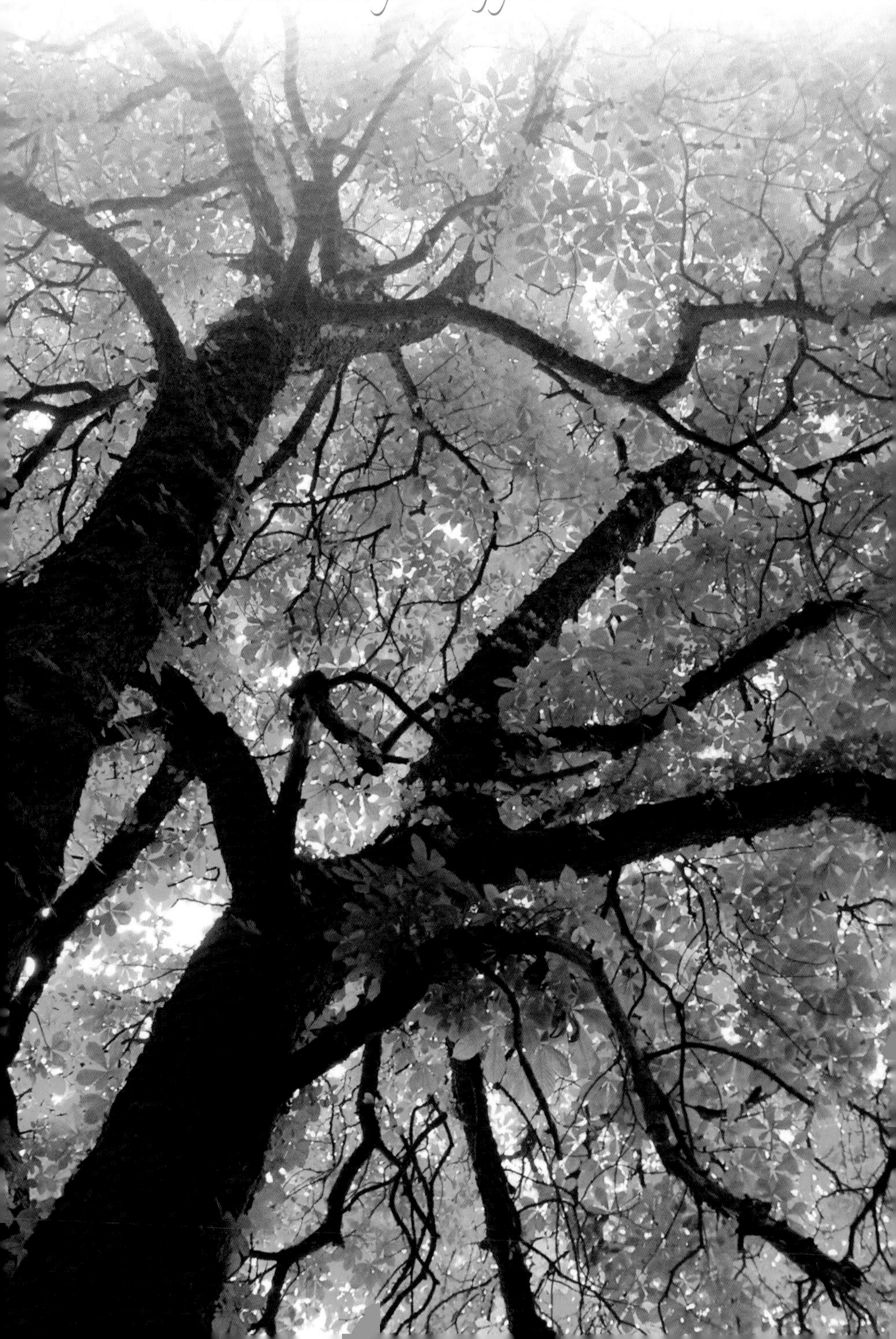

emergency services, and in professions such as the police and the law.

This said, they have a tendency to suppress their identity, their true, emotional nature, for the benefit of others. However, this can lead to self-destructive, extreme, and stubborn behavior. Once a path or goal has been chosen, they will not change their minds, even if they come to realize that their chosen route will not produce the desired result and it would be better to choose again. For their own benefit, Horse chestnut-born people should learn to be honest with themselves and sometimes lighten up with a little humor (but not cynicism or sarcasm) and learn to laugh at themselves when need be. This will bring healing and gradually their true nature will come to the fore once more. It is okay for their life path to be easy every now and then, they don't have to choose the most difficult way forward to be of use to others.

In a nutshell

Horse chestnut-born people should learn that when taking important decisions they must ask themselves: "Am I really making these choices to make myself happy or am I trying to meet the expectations of others, whether it is my parents or my boss?" They should recognize that it is also a sign of maturity to admit mistakes and wrong turns rather than hanging on until the bitter end. Having goals gives people a sense of security and purpose in life, so they should learn to choose these carefully, and not to feel constrained or limited but to "think big."

As the old saying has it "laughter is the best medicine," and laughing at yourself and at life can provide relief for self-critical Horse chestnut-born people and heal old wounds. It is important for them to get a sense of when their straightforward and direct approach is appropriate and helpful, and when it puts pressure on people and crosses their boundaries.

Healing powers

The seeds, bark, leaves, and blossom of the Horse chestnut provide active ingredients for the pharmaceutical industry, which uses them to prepare various treatments. These include preparations to support the veins and anti-inflammatory treatments for stomach ulcers, ulcerative colitis, and hemorrhoids.

Birth-tree power

The authentic power of pure humor.

Inspiration from a Horse chestnut personality

We are responsible for what we do, but also for what we neglect to do.

Voltaire
French writer, and forerunner of the French Revolution

Ash

May 25–June 3 and November 22–December 1

Element family: Air

Gifts and talents

Unconventional, robust, impulsive, full of energy; conciliatory, capable of extraordinary achievements, with a healing gift; travel enthusiasts; creative and artistic, inspirational, and encouragingly supportive of others.

Carpe arborem

By giving expression to my creativity, I find trust in my strength, which creates healing in me and around me.

Symbolism

The Celts attributed to the Ash the power both to summon rain and to contain and to counteract the often destructive power of water. Thanks to their extensive and very dense root systems, Ash trees are still used today as a natural way to stabilize embankments. As the wood of the Ash is both tough and flexible, it was used to make bows and spears, so the tree became a symbol of the defense of personal freedom.

The Ash path through life

Ash-born people belong to the family of Air elements, which brings them the inspiring lightheartedness with which they dance through life and their infectious joie-de-vivre. They have seemingly inexhaustible reserves of energy and are bursting with vitality, a dynamic that informs all their relationships. The words "calm" and "rest" seem completely alien to them, especially when young. Many of the people around them and with whom they come into contact welcome this trait, although some, especially those

who have less energy and find it difficult to make changes in their lives, are more resistant to it.

Just as a river flows and creates new paths, the itchy feet of these free spirits see them crossing continents, either as solo travelers or as group leaders, seeking greater independence on both a material and spiritual plane. This is one reason why Ash-born people are often drawn to working for themselves, or they will find a profession in which they can have as much latitude as possible for their creative ideas and can take decisions independently. The sky is the limit for their professional choices, from singer and actor to top-level sports people and healers.

Ash personalities are always ready to break away from anything that might slow them down or hinder their progress, as they long for variety in life and embrace the rollercoaster ride of their world of strong emotions. In order to avoid being held back by any pent-up anger and the self-destructive behavior it can engender, they should make a conscious decision to "lay down their weapons" and instead learn to channel this strong energy into creative or healing activities. They must recognize that their (personal) responsibility for their own lives will develop in parallel with their increasing independence. This is how they will learn to accept responsibility (and the associated consequences) for their thoughts, emotions, and actions.

Ash-born people usually seem to have little or no time for the so-called small things in life, such as cleaning. However, while they may be rather chaotic and lack structure in their lives, they often prove to be remarkable leaders. They create balance within a group and are good at spotting the potential of individual group members. When focused on a common goal with the the combined strength of a group behind them, Ash-born people can achieve the kind of extraordinary things that would be beyond their reach when acting alone.

In a nutshell

Just as the wood of the Ash is strong yet flexible, one of the lessons Ash-born people must learn is to stop slavishly adhering to old habits and established ways of behavior so they too can be flexible and adapt to whatever life sends their way. If they don't, they will be limiting the options that are available to them and the freedoms and ease that come with those opportunities.

When implementing projects and ideas, Ash-born people should learn to direct and use the group to its full advantage; this will enable them to achieve almost anything—even the most seemingly unattainable of goals will be achievable for the benefit of everyone. They should channel their great energy in constructive ways (for example, in sport, art, or healing) rather than falling prey to (self-)destructive behavior. Anger and aggression are merely an expression of the suppressed opposite of creativity, vitality, and pure inventiveness.

Healing powers

Preprations made from the Ash tree are effective against gout and rheumatism, help cleanse the blood, heal wounds, and are diuretic and purgative; Ash seeds help to support the liver and spleen.

Birth-tree power

The compelling power of independence.

Inspiration from an Ash personality

We cannot direct the wind, but we can adjust the sails.

John F. Kennedy, 35th president of the United States

Hornbeam

June 4–13 and December 2–11

Element family: Fire

Gifts and talents
A strong sense of justice and responsibility; an esthete, confident, sensitive, disciplined, and reliable; a pugnacious persistence, robust, hardworking, and realistic.

Carpe arborem
I activate with compassion the power within me that is able to heal all judgment created by my mind.

Symbolism
For the Celts, the wood of the Hornbeam, also known as White beech (due to its pale wood) or Ironwood, was one of the magical woods (along with Elder and Hazel) associated with the wise women. When Christianity was introduced in Western Europe, with their connection to the wisdom of the Goddess and their knowledge of herbs, these women took on the role of healers. However, they were persecuted and burned as associates of the Devil and witches. A living hedge of Hornbeam will protect a house on both the physical and energetic levels, and represent a symbolic border between the visible and the invisible worlds at the same time. With its great durability and hardness, the wood came to be known colloquially as "musclewood."

The Hornbeam path through life
Hornbeam-born people belong to the family of Fire elements, the source of their great drive and positive attitude. They are very grounded and dominant, and could almost be said to be carved out of solid wood themselves. Along with Pine and Hazel,

The natural power of universal justice

Hornbeam is one of the most resilient trees in the Celtic tree horoscope. Its gift is being able to focus exclusively on the positive aspects of life and to perceive the meaning and the greater natural order behind the events that take place. Horn-beam people are consequently able to view a setback, including one that other people might consider a terrible stroke of fate, merely as just another of life's challenges that they can ultimately turn to their advantage. They can generally derive some benefit from challenging life events because Hornbeam personalities usually recognize at an early age that it is not external circumstances and situations that are able to break people's will, but rather themselves if they cease to believe in their own gifts and talents. This attitude to life earns Hornbeam-born people the admiration of their peers, which they are fully capable of enjoying to the utmost.

Horn-beam born people draw strength from the natural world, which they should try to bring into every aspect of their lives. If they succeed in mastering the transition from the judgmental mind to the compassionate heart, they will become healers, both for themselves and for their fellow human beings. They are always ready to listen to other people's problems and are generally able to come up with useful advice, sometimes suggesting the kind of left field "fix" that can produce amazing results.

With all their talents, Hornbeam personalities usually find employment in industries where their esthetic sense can be put to good use (such as designer, stylist, interior decorator, or landscape architect), or in professions involving the law, such as in the legal or financial systems. However, if their idea of justice does not coincide with the laws currently in force, they are not afraid to question and denounce them.

In a nutshell

The lesson that resilient Hornbeam-born people need to learn is to be kind and receptive to the emotional world of their fellow human beings, and to stand by and support them in word and deed with their positive outlook on life. They should recognize that there is no ultimate justice, nor should they try to dispense their own notion of justice. The key is not to make judgments with the head but rather with the compassion of the heart, to find new and creative solutions that will benefit everyone concerned. They are very adept at maintaining and defending their personal boundaries but may also learn how to reveal their feelings to other people, who often regard them as something of a mystery.

Healing powers

Hornbeam is a medicinal plant used in Bach Flower Remedies to counteract excessive fatigue and exhaustion, and in traditional medicine to treat white skin spots (vitiligo) according to Hildegard of Bingen.

Birth-tree power

The natural power of universal justice.

Inspiration from a Hornbeam personality

The intellect is constantly afraid. Essentially, it is only afraid of one thing: the heart—the intellect is used within the body only as a servant but it has managed to become the master. But the actual master is the heart.

Osho

Indian spiritual leader and founder of the neo-Sannyasi movement

Fig Tree

June 14–23 and December 12–21

Element family: Earth

Carpe arborem
The peace and harmony of Nature inspire as well as stimulate my creativity.

Gifts and talents
Relaxed, Nature-loving, a focus of peace; cosmopolitan, tolerant, intuitive; hard-working, sensitive, imaginative and creative; ready to give, quick on the uptake, seeking a sense of security, and family-oriented.

Symbolism
In many cultures, the Fig tree is a symbol of happiness and prosperity; in the Bible, it becomes a representation of our spiritual peace, just as it is viewed as the tree of enlightenment in Buddhism.

The Fig tree path through life
Fig tree-born people belong to the family of Earth elements, which is the source of their groundedness, their deep love of Nature, and their inner peace. Their peers therefore often see them as a safe haven, as people they feel safe to be around. The Fig tree's sensitive nature endows people with this birth-tree with a perceptive, intuitive, and creative inner life. They need to be allowed the space in which to develop their emotional expression in inventive ways in the artistic and creative fields. Because of their fear of being hurt, they generally hide their soft interiors behind a mask that can often be cool and distant, or numb their senses with various stimulants and distractions. If they can tap

The imaginative power of sensitivity and creativity

into their emotions and their inner peace, they can greatly enrich the lives of those around them.

Fig tree-born people like to dive deep into life with all their senses and always make the most of any sensuous, esthetic, and cultural experiences they have. As a result, they are often faced with the challenge of moderating their behavior, particularly when vacillating between two extremes, such as in relation to food, exercise, work, leisure time, and much more besides. For them, being in control of their lives means finding the right level in all its aspects and maintaining a balance between being active and passive.

Fig tree-born folk are real people magnets. They enjoy being at the center of the large circle of friends and acquaintances that gather around them. In times of crisis or when problems arise, their friends turn to them first as they are by nature patient peacemakers, always ready to listen.

Family-oriented Fig tree personalities like nothing better than to look after their loved ones. They have a tendency always to be at the beck and call of those around them, their family and friends, doing their utmost for them until feeling tired and worn out. The people around them may ultimately react to their well-meant over-attentiveness with annoyance or anger, and many will even exploit it.

Fig tree people have a great need for harmony and so try to avoid all and any conflict by bottling up negative emotions, which then fester inside them.

Whether working as an artist, a farmer, or a chef or cook, Fig tree-born people have many options in life thanks to their skill with their hands and their enthusiasm; if they were to have a motto, it would undoubtedly be "with people and for people." Hence they will bring peace and harmony to the world with diplomacy and imagination, wherever life may happen to take them. Athough people with this birth-tree are always heading out into the big, wide world, they always love to come back to their warm and comfortable homes and to their loved ones. They derive their strength from the natural world and their families, finding a sense of security for which they have a longing deep within.

In a nutshell

Conflict happens and as such should be acceptable; just as a storm clears the air, it is entirely natural and part of life. For Fig tree-born people, the important thing in this respect is to recognize and acknowledge their feelings with honesty, as this will ease their minds, while also enabling them to bring about change in a situation. Finding emotional balance is a top priority for Fig tree-born people. To keep up their energy reserves or recharge their batteries, they must look after themselves and learn how to satisfy their own needs first by expressing their creative natures.

Healing powers

The white sap of the Fig tree is used to soothe insect bites and to remove warts. The fruits of the Fig have antibacterial properties, strengthen the liver, and help with constipation, ulcers, and also skin rashes.

Birth-tree power

The imaginative power of sensitivity and creativity.

Inspiration from a Fig tree personality

If we dream alone, it will generally remain a dream; but when many people have the same dream, it is the beginning of a new reality.

Friedensreich Hundertwasser
Austrian artist and self-proclaimed "doctor of architecture"

Birch

Element family: Water

Gifts and talents

A strong belief in community; helpful and modest, with a charismatic aura; confident, ambitious, relaxed, resilient, self-critical, with a sense of duty and responsibility; wise and intuitive.

Carpe arborem

I am the bearer of light, bringing light to you, to free you and those around you from burdens and unconscious torments of the soul.

Symbolism

The third day after the summer solstice, which marks the longest day and shortest night of the year, is the day of the Birch. In many cultures, it is a magic tree that is capable of warding off evil. It is the first tree in the Celtic tree alphabet, representing new beginnings and an ascent to a higher plane. The Birch supports magic and is a symbol of joy, beauty, and the creative power of love, of which its heart-shaped leaves are a reminder.

The Birch tree path through life

Birch-born people belong to the family of Water elements, the source of their empathetic and protective natures. When Birch personalities enter a room, for those present it is as though the sun is just rising, caressing them gently with its invigorating and warming rays. They bring light to the human heart with their graceful and charismatic aura. With their deep sense of gratitude for life itself, Birch-born people are an inspiration and source of support for their fellows, happy to serve in communities that have set positive goals.

The light-bringing power
of grateful humility

They feel most at home in the small and familiar circle of their families, although it is here—among those they know best—that they are also required to relinquish their strong need for control and (self-)criticism and give free rein to all their emotions again. More than anything else, they could usefully learn not to "hide their light under a bushel" and shine only for others, but finally learn to praise themselves for their outstanding achievements, even if at first they fail to recognize them as such.

Birch tree personalities bring their fellow human beings strength and support, helping them to find different solutions in difficult situations in life.

They are born leaders with a big heart and a sharp mind, and their exceptional qualities can be brought to bear in all socially committed professions, from nursery and school teaching to helping the dying and managing large organizations that work for the public good.

In a nutshell

The lesson for Birch-born people is to learn to distance themselves more from the personal and generally highly emotional dramas in their lives. However, they will not achieve this by retreating into themselves and making important decisions using their intellect alone, but instead by opening up their hearts and releasing the healing power of empathy once more, for themselves and for those around them.

Whether professionally or within their family, it is the very nature of Birch-born people that sets processes in motion, starting to shake things up and break away from old and ingrained habits, and shines a light on whatever is hidden. Another lesson for them to learn is that of letting go or, to put it another way, giving up control and being able to trust instead.

Their need to control and protect everything will gradually diminish as they learn to let go and trust life.

Healing powers

Birch leaf tea and sap are used in natural beauty tonics and have stimulant properties for the gall bladder and kidneys; they can boost the mood and encourage mental flexibility. Other ingredients from the Birch are also used in homeopathy.

Birth-tree power

The light-bringing power of grateful humility.

Inspiration from a Birch personality

In future, modern research will have to align itself more closely with the human conscience than it has previously.

Victor F Hess
Austrian-American physicist and 1934 Nobel Prize laureate
for the discovery of cosmic rays

June 24—Saint John's Day

Apple Tree

June 25–July 4 and December 23–January 1

Element family: Earth

Gifts and talents

Sensitive, helpful, patient, open to unconditional love, sympathetic; attentive, giving, charming, intuitive, and full of ideas; creates balance; a positive and charismatic aura.

Carpe arborem

I create balance and harmony with love and empathy for myself and for others.

Symbolism

In most cultures, the Apple tree is a symbol of love, fertility, and insight, as well an an indicator of inner wealth. For the Celts, it was one of the sacred trees, symbolizing love and immortality. An old Celtic legend tells of an Apple tree standing in Avalon, the Celtic paradise, whose fruits bestow immortality.

The Apple tree path through life

Apple tree-born people belong to the family of Earth elements, which gives them the ability to mediate between others with empathy. With their message of unconditional love, highly charismatic Apple tree personalities are constantly seeking out ways of uniting people and bringing them together rather than dividing and judging them. In this respect, they are helped by their ability to recognize and highlight the essential things that people have in common with a view to achieving greater understanding. They bring the gift of love and a sense of security, and are always ready to give themselves entirely and wholeheartedly. Like the Fig tree, the Yew, or even the Elm, their energy is finely balanced,

The uniting power of unconditional love

so it is important for them to learn how to set boundaries at the right time and in a loving way. This also means being able to say no at times in order to look after their own physical and mental well-being.

In this respect, Apple tree-born people are constantly being tested by the world around them, being faced with the challenge of identifying where boundaries lie and recognizing that sometimes sacrifice for others has little to do with love. If sacrifice means they start to feel drained or even ill, they will no longer have the strength to help their fellow human beings.

In a nutshell
The lesson for Apple tree people is to learn not to seek love and recognition in the world around them, either in the workplace or among friends and family. If they do, they can fall prey to the emotional ups and downs of those around them, which can end up being a real drain on them emotionally, too. The solution is to find the source of love and self-love within themselves. In this way Apple tree people can find an emotional balance and be in a position to instill understanding on both sides when there is conflict between people.

Healing powers
Apples boost the metabolism, stimulating blood formation, detoxification and fat management, while also regulating the digestion. Tea made from apple peel has antipyretic properties, harmonizes the nervous system, and boosts bladder and kidney function.

Birth-tree power
The uniting power of unconditional love.

No matter how close two human beings may be, there is always a gulf between them which only love can bridge, and that only from hour to hour.

Hermann Hesse
German author and poet

June 25–July 4 and December 23–January 1

Fir

January 2–11 and July 5–14

Element family: Water

Gifts and talents

Forward-looking, self-confident, and searching; reliable, highly sympathetic; good at setting boundaries; very perceptive; spontaneous and creative; a protector, an extraordinary aura; very circumspect, demanding, and independent.

Carpe arborem

I summon the courage to show my vulnerability and so regain my trust in myself and in life little by little.

Symbolism

As the "queen of the forest," as the mighty Fir was known to the Celtic people, it was a symbol of beauty, great majesty, and far-sightedness.

The Fir path through life

Fir-born people belong to the family of Water elements, which is the source of their flexible organizational skills and profound trust in life itself. They radiate grace, dignity and self-assurance, although this can be why others perceive them as unapproachable, distant, and perhaps even a little arrogant. However, behind the cool exterior of these born leaders lurks a generous and highly sensitive heart filled with love and ready to give. The challenge for Fir personalities is to open up this big heart to themselves as well as to others, so they can learn to consciously get in touch with themselves and their emotions once more. In so doing, they will gain ever greater trust in the natural flow of life.

The protective power of (primordial) trust

Fir personalities need great courage to go against their own nature and tear down their supposedly "protective" walls; they also use these walls to shut themselves off from the love and empathy of those they love most and for whom they long so much. However, when they gather the confidence and dare to make the leap into the unplumbed depths of their emotions, they will recognize the true part they can play and become a shining example of what confidence can achieve for their fellows.

Fir personalities are not frightened of taking on responsibility. Blessed with many different qualities, they are suited to any profession that involves attention to detail and a high degree of complexity—all doors are open to them, from managing a catering firm to school administrator. The focus should always be on making the most of their creativity and flair for human contact; under no circumstances should these talents be neglected.

In a nutshell

Fear is all that separates Fir-born people from the depth of their emotional world and its associated aspects of compassion and sensitivity and their basic trust in life. Their lesson is to learn to reestablish contact with their feelings and to communicate them (or give them creative expression) so that they can gradually begin to get in touch with their emotions again. In this respect, their fear of losing control over their emotions holds them back. The solution is to be aware of this fear and not to fight it but to work through it. In this way, inner conflict can be resolved, along with any feelings of stagnation and being stuck in a rut, and they will be able to move on in life once more, full of trust.

Healing powers

Essential oil extracted from the resin, needles, and buds of the fir tree is used to treat bronchitis, gout, rheumatism, and sore throats. The wood, needles, and resin of the fir can be burned as incense to purify a room.

Birth-tree power

The protective power of (primordial) trust.

Inspiration from a Fir personality

To understand the heart and mind of person, look not at what he has already achieved but at what he aspires to.

Khalil Gibran
Lebanese-American poet and philosopher

Elm

Element family: Water

Gifts and talents
A positive aura; creative, altruistic, social, tolerant; resolute, positive, realistic, tough, strong-willed, and just; individual, consciousness-raising, magnanimous, helpful, and full of vitality.

Carpe arborem
I acknowledge my fears and use them as a way to discover my worth and the light within me. With faith in myself, I begin to act with courage.

Symbolism
Regarded by the Celts as a herald of Nature and burgeoning spring, the Elm, or *Ulmus* in Latin, has become a symbol of awakening consciousness.

The Elm path through life
Elm-born people belong to the family of Water elements, the source of their considerable creative powers. This talent for creative self-expression enriches their experiences, which they live to the full and the fruits of which they pass on to others. The role of Elm-born personalities is to give free rein to their emotions in their own particular and imaginative way in whatever they do, whether working in the arts or with people of any age group. They serve their fellow human beings by passing on the wealth of their experience and their innate wisdom.

The challenge that every Elm personality faces is to strike the right balance between giving and taking. They should also carefully weigh up their reasons for giving and the hopes and

The creative power of self-worth

expectations they attach to the outcome. It is only when they are prepared to give wholeheartedly and instinctively and for the benefit of everyone, that they will receive back what they give, many times over, albeit in ways they could not have anticipated.

As they become more able to make use of their creativity, Elm-born people develop a growing awareness of the light within them, becoming radiant personalities capable of touching and moving people deep in their hearts.

In a nutshell
Throughout their lives, Elm-born people frequently ask themselves "Will I ever be good enough?" Their lack of self-worth causes their minds to race constantly, allowing no rest. They set standards for themselves and others that are too high, leading to constant disappointment in life. Their lesson is to find their own worth through creative, inventive self-expression; they are best able to serve their fellow human beings and the world in general when they are doing what they love.

Healing powers
Thanks to its wound-healing and blood-cleansing properties, Slippery Elm bark powder can be used to treat chronic rashes, abscesses, gout, rheumatism, fever, and internal bleeding.

Birth-tree power
The creative power of self-worth.

Inspiration from an Elm personality

Our deepest fear is not that we are inadequate. Our deepest fear is that we are powerful beyond measure. It is our light, not our darkness, that most frightens us. We ask ourselves, who am I to be brilliant, gorgeous, talented and fabulous? Actually, who are you not to be? You are a child of God. . . . We were born to make manifest the glory of God that is within us. It's not just in some of us, it's in everyone. . . . As we are liberated from our own fear, our presence automatically liberates others.

Nelson Mandela
former anti-apartheid fighter, first Black president of South Africa,
and Nobel Peace Prize laureate

Cypress

Element family: Air

Gifts and talents

Inquisitive, noble, and intuitive; forward-thinking, active, highly individual; positive, sociable, independent, inventive, successful; secretive; a lover of art and culture; brave and daring.

Carpe arborem

I allow the light within me more and more space. I dare to reach my goals with clarity, and so gain ever greater inner freedom.

Symbolism

The Cypress is the sun worshiper of the tree world. It tapers to a point and stands straight and tall in the Mediterranean land-scape, like a signpost pointing up to the sky. In mythology, it is a symbol of the immortality of the soul and of life after death.

The Cypress path through life

Cypress-born people belong to the family of Air elements, the source of their individuality and independence. The paths their lives take are generally far from the "norm," but essentially have one thing in common—they very seldom take the direct route to achieving their ultimate life goal of being admirable, inde-pendent, and successful. They are easily sidetracked, lured down different paths that seem far more interesting to them by comparison, meeting exceptional and memorable people and making fascinating discoveries that they would otherwise have missed. They are susceptible to the nagging feeling that they are missing out on something exciting.

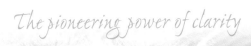
The pioneering power of clarity

As a result of this adventurous and highly creative approach to life, in the form of the detours that they take along the way, Cypress people amass a great wealth of experience that ultimately helps them to achieve their ambitions. With "the way is the goal" very much at the forefront of their minds, they like to live life to the full, with all its emotional rollercoasters. They are true connoisseurs of art, culture, gastronomy, and, of course, have a love of the Mediterranean climate.

Just as Cypress personalities have a great need for the sun physically, and love to feel its warmth on their back whenever they have the opportunity, they also need to feel a sense of security and acceptance from their companions. Having a goal and clarity about where they are going in life is essential for them. They live openly and courageously, always heading toward the light with a profound belief that life only takes place in the here and now, in the present moment. For them life is to be consciously enjoyed, in all its amazing richness, and to be celebrated anew every day.

In terms of their professional lives, they seek a career in which they can work independently, often interacting with people from all walks of life and cultures. Cypress personalities are therefore often found in professions that are linked with art, culture, and gastronomy, such as the travel industry or as museum guides, or even musicians and chefs.

In a nutshell

Standing out at all costs can turn into an obsession and suggests a need for inner freedom. But in order to achieve the feeling of freedom that Elm-born people desire so much, first they must separate themselves from their concept of freedom.

Their task is to learn to recognize that by resisting established practices and social mores, whether in the form of laws or the unwritten rules that govern the way people live together, all they are doing is using up vital energy. They must learn to abide by

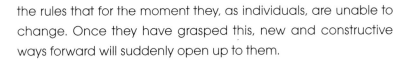

the rules that for the moment they, as individuals, are unable to change. Once they have grasped this, new and constructive ways forward will suddenly open up to them.

Healing powers

Teas, tinctures, and essential oils made from the twigs, fruits, and wood of the Cypress are useful in treating colds, hemorrhoids, and conditions affecting the womb.

Birth-tree power

The pioneering power of clarity.

Inspiration from Cypress personalities

The angels are always present with a piece of music such as this.

The heart ennobles the person.

Wolfgang Amadeus Mozart
Austrian composer

In all chaos there is a cosmos, in all disorder a secret.

Everything that irritates us about others can lead us to an understanding of ourselves.

Carl Gustav Jung
Swiss psychiatrist and founder
of analytical psychology

January 25–February 3 and July 26–August 4

Poplar

February 4–8 and August 5–13

Element family: Ether

Gifts and talents

Intuitive, sensitive, vulnerable, and patient; a lover of Nature and travel, with a great thirst for knowledge; realistic, ambitious, enterprising, questioning, understanding, frugal; a seeker of knowledge.

Carpe arborem

I intuitively recognize the essence, the true being behind all outward appearances.

Symbolism

Poplar was described as the tree of the people by the Celts, probably because it played an important part in their daily lives simply as a means for survival; for example they would make shoes and shields from its soft, flexible wood. The Druids are said to have heard messages from the spiritual world in the rustling of its leaves.

The Poplar path through life

Poplar-born people belong to the family of Ether elements, which gives them the gifts of perception and empathy, an instinctive understanding of people's feelings, along with an unquenchable thirst for knowledge and insight. They read between the lines and can see through deceptive outward appearances; they know "which way the wind is blowing" and in conversation are good at intuiting what is really being said. However, this gift also presents them with the challenge of being equally clear about their own emotions and underlying needs. Without this clarity, they tend toward mixed emotions, with the result that they

The grounding power of being

are more sensitive to the feelings of those around them than their own. At some point, they start to lose track of why they are subject to such strong mood swings—and especially how to deal with them. The upshot is that they constantly feel on edge as they go about their everyday lives.

As far as material possessions are concerned, Poplar-born people are generally very frugal. They recognize at an early age that in life it is not all about having a quick answer ready to hand, it is often far more important to ask the right questions at the right time. What drives them on is their quest for greater insight, a deeper understanding of the interconnectedness of all things. This is demonstrated in their great thirst for knowledge and experience, which they seek to satisfy by reading books, or attending lectures and seminars, or even traveling to different countries.

It is important for Poplar personalities to put all the knowledge and insights they acquire to good use in their lives. This will help them to keep their feet on the ground and not to lose touch with reality. While they may feel free and entirely at home up there in the lofty heights of their ivory tower, they need an earthly, grounded counterpoint to give them some balance. They can find this in the natural world, whether pottering in the garden, taking long walks, or enjoying meditative silence in the countryside. This all helps them to maintain their equilibrium, even when going through deep emotional lows. Poplar personalities are adept at remaining flexible, recognizing when they have to "go with the flow" or bend a little in the face of life's storms in order not to be hurt. To support themselves mentally and physically, they should learn to quietly take a step back more often, to better reflect on the intense emotions provoked by the day's events and to consciously work through them.

Poplar-born people are able to develop their talents particularly well in those professions that require an intuitive sensitivity; this opens the door to a wide range of options in professional teaching environments, the field of psychology, and in roles requiring strong leadership skills.

In a nutshell
Poplar-born people's lesson is to learn to ask themselves the right question at the right time, something they are already adept at doing in relation to other people. Rather than answering the important questions with their head, they should sense the way forward with their heart. Placing too much emphasis on ambition and the need to prove themselves will bring these sensitive souls to their knees. They must recognize that self-worth is not defined by achievements, it is more important that they use their gift for bringing people together and support them with compassion.

Healing powers
The bark and leaves of the Poplar are used to treat pain and rheumatism. Birch leaf tea has a purifying effect and Birch leaf ointment can be used to treat sunburn, psoriasis, as well as neurodermatitis.

Birth-tree power
The grounding power of being.

Inspiration from a Poplar personality
Anything one man can imagine, other men can make real.

The earth does not need new continents, but new men.

I dream with my eyes open.

Jules Verne
French author

Cedar of Lebanon

February 9–18 and August 14–23

Element family: Ether

Gifts and talents

Highly receptive to the idea of change, headstrong, autonomous, communicative; born leaders, self-confident, with great patience and persistence; dignified, tolerant, courageous, and graceful; successful, individual, pugnacious; creative and sensitive to beauty.

Carpe arborem

I am freedom of choice, the core from which the creative powers in my life can take effect. I free myself from the limitations of my understanding with humility and reinvent myself over and over again.

Symbolism

For the Celts the Cedar was "the tree of kings and enlightenment." With their stately and graceful forms, Cedars have long been a symbol of grandeur and dignity, both in the Bible and in the Celtic tradition. And with their pleasant and beguiling scent, they are also associated with the world of the senses.

The Cedar path through life

Cedar-born people belong to the family of Ether elements, the source of their empathetic and intuitive manner in communicating with people and bringing them together.

Even at an early age, Cedar-born people generally prove to be adept at handling life well, and not just because of their strong sense of creativity and sensitivity to beauty—they also have a great willingness and capacity for change. Deep inside, they feel that life is all about constant change and progression,

moving forward. Their task is to learn to accept this change with gratitude as it will bring them new perspectives and make them aware of what is essential in their lives. Once they have recognized this and put it into practice, they will easily and gracefully be able to shake off and leave behind whatever is at once both old and outmoded.

Filled with energy, they set off for pastures new in pursuit of their vision, where, with sufficient patience and perseverance, they almost always achieve their goal. In doing so they should not allow setbacks or criticism to knock them off course, and if they can learn to ignore these difficulties, they will instead prove to be valuable experiences.

The driving force behind Cedar personalities is a desire to create something new with and for people, bearing in mind the maxim "We are doing great things together here." Hence, they can best use their talents in those professions that connect people creatively in a variety of ways and unite them in pursuing a common goal, in any area of life. It is also important that their chosen profession will allow them plenty of leeway for making their own decisions and acting independently. The pleasure they take in variety and diversity can turn their lives into something of an adventure, and they dive deep, making the most of their experiences and all that life has to offer. In doing so they are constantly being challenged to trust, to rise above their reservations and doubts and to choose to let go rather than to hold on tight. This is where their knack for living life well comes into play, a constant asset on their journey.

Deep inside, Cedar-born people sense that if they want to make a difference in the world, they have to begin with themselves. The changes they want to see outside must first take place within them, before these changes can be extended to the world around them.

In a nutshell

In general, Cedar personalities have a tendency toward excess, to going "over the top"—especially in their speech—so they should learn to concentrate on what is essential, what really matters. They find it hard to deal with criticism, firstly because they are very critical of themselves, but also because it knocks their self-esteem. They should learn not to derive their sense of self-worth from the world around them and the way their achievements are perceived. They should recognize that they can only value themselves by accepting themselves as they are, something they often find difficult. When they learn to stop judging themelves, in other words, to adopt a non-judgmental perspective, they will become increasingly aware that there is no "better" or "worse," no "right" or "wrong."

Healing powers

When burned as incense, wood from the Cedar of Lebanon promotes courage and self-confidence.

Birth-tree power

The transformational power of enlightenment.

Inspiration from a Cedar personality

You cannot find yourself by going into the past. You find yourself by coming into the present.

Eckhart Tolle
spiritual teacher

Pine

February 19–29 and August 24–September 2

Element family: Fire

Gifts and talents

Patient, cautious, careful, with a gift for observation; sensible, self-assured, eloquent; organized, economical, encouraging, adaptable, and frugal.

Carpe arborem

Patience and adaptability give me strength, while communication is my way into my feelings, the lifeblood that allows me to achieve what no one else can.

Symbolism

Pine, a family of conifers in the genus Pinus, is a symbol of persistence and modesty in many cultures. Thanks to its ability to grow in a variety of different conditions, the "tree of fire," as it was known to the Celtic people, has become established in a number of forms around the world.

The Pine path through life

Pine-born people belong to the family of Fire elements, which gives them adaptability and the ability to communicate well with others. People with this birth-tree can feel at home almost anywhere in the world, without feeling the need to make many demands. They do not view a move, whether to another town, country, or even continent, as any great challenge. They have a thirst for life, deep within, that drives them on and keeps them going, however adverse circumstances may become.

At heart, they are spirited or even temperamental, but as Pine-born people balance this out with a strong and practical mind,

The persistent power of patient observation of life

this forceful, emotional side to their character is usually kept in check and they are not normally perceived as being temperamental by outsiders.

Striking a balance between the head and heart is one of Pine-born people's greatest challenges. The solution is to transform their feelings through the power of Fire, which means that anger may also be expressed. However, if they are not able to do so, which is often the case with children who have had a very strict upbringing, they may overcompensate for this in other ways.

The parents of a child brought up in such a way may think that child well-adjusted and well-behaved, but later think their child may reveal itself to be a "walking timebomb," or the suppression of anger may later reveal itself in self-destructive (autoagressive) behavior.

Once Pine-born people have "checked out" their surroundings using their astute talent for observation, they make the most of their eloquence to attract the attention of those around them, encouraged by the energy of their audience. Their talent for being adaptable does not lie in pretense or surrendering to the wishes of others. Being adaptable also means taking a creative, flexible, and proactive approach at all times—as opposed to just reacting to people and events unconsciously. In this way, Pine-born people learn to get a better sense of and to be more aware of themselves by recognizing and expressing their emotions. With their talents, they are often found in the teaching and entertainment industries (such as cabaret artists and singers), although they are also well represented in the technical professions as well. When choosing a career, they should make sure that their talent for communication can be used in a variety of ways.

In a nutshell

Pine-born people should learn to give themselves the space in which to express their feelings, which they are best able to do by using their creativity and communication skills. They often struggle

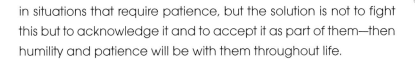

in situations that require patience, but the solution is not to fight this but to acknowledge it and to accept it as part of them—then humility and patience will be with them throughout life.

Healing powers
The needles and resin of the Pine tree have properties that help to clear the mind and revitalize the body in cases of flu and asthma.

Birth-tree power
The persistent power of patient observation of life.

Inspiration from a Pine personality

Knowing is not enough—we must apply. Willing is not enough—we must do.

A man who no longer loves and no longer errs should have himself buried.

Johann Wolfgang von Goethe
German poet, who conducted research and published on
a wide range of scientific topics

Willow

March 1–10 and September 3–12

Element family: Water

Gifts and talents

Flexible, energetic, with great tolerance and perseverance; intuitive, adaptable, and capable; spontaneous, Nature-loving, enthusiastic; robust, tough, emotional, pioneering, and sensitive.

Carpe arborem

I respect my boundaries and those of my fellow human beings, and let my feelings and the flow of life take its course.

Symbolism

In many cultures the Willow is a symbol of fertility and vital power. Its branches are used to make divining (dowsing) rods, which can detect water hidden below ground.

The Willow path through life

Willow-born people belong to the family of Water elements, the source of their vitality and tolerance. Provided they don't try to neglect or suppress any important aspects of their life path, they will essentially enjoy a robust, adaptable, and strong nature. Willow trees need the element of Water more than any other in the Celtic tree horoscope, just as people with this birth-tree need a connection to their emotional side and to consciously accept and express all their feelings.

This also puts them in touch with their subconscious, their deep inner feelings. They are able to tap into their previous experiences and use them to further their personal development quite easily, even intuitively. However, if they choose to ignore their sensitive side and close their hearts to protect themselves from pain and

The vitalizing power of tolerance

suffering, they will lose their vitality and ability to adapt and be flexible. As a result, they may become stubborn and intolerant, leading to feelings of frustration and even depression. But they can find healing in Nature and through daily physical exercise, which will keep their bodies supple and distract them from negative emotions, prompting empathy and compassion, both for themselves and those around them. Drawing on their natural desire for physical activity, they should choose careers that give them sufficient opportunity to move their bodies, ideally outside in the fresh air and in the company of other people, whom they can help with their activity.

In a nutshell

Willow-born people push the limits emotionally and physically and have a tendency to exhaust themselves as a result, leading to both mental and physical burnout. As their great energy generally allows them to pick themselves back up, they often go through this cycle several times in their lives before they are finally ready to learn from it. The solution is to be found in the timely recognition and respecting, not just of their own boundaries, but also those of others, who may otherwise ride roughshod over Willow-born people. Any form of sporting activity or involvement with Nature can help to allow Willow personalities to let off steam.

Healing powers

Salicin is found in the bark of the Willow and is synthesized in the form of aspirin, which has an analgesic effect, in rheumatic diseases especially. It also reduces fever, soothes headaches, and helps with kidney and bladder complaints. However, a side-effect to be aware of is that salicin can also irritate and attack the stomach lining.

Birth-tree power

The vitalizing power of tolerance.

Everyone wants to change the world, but no one is willing to change himself.

Leo Tolstoy
Russian author and anarchist

March 1–10 and September 3–12

Linden Tree (Bee Tree)

March 11–20 and September 13–22

Element family: Water

Gifts and talents

Sensitive, loyal, understanding; artistically and philosophically gifted; just and fair when bringing balance to situations, diplomatic; (self-)critical, loyal, helpful, cheerful, and sociable.

Carpe arborem

In recognizing and setting my own boundaries, my heart will open fearlessly to give joyfully.

Symbolism

With the shape of a heart echoed in both the leaves and the silhouette of a mature Linden tree, it is a symbol of maternal care, love, and empathy, both for ourselves and our fellow human beings. It represents calm, the resolution of disagreements and conflict, and the restoration of harmony. For the Slav, Germanic, and Celtic peoples, it is therefore venerated as a tree of law and justice, and in centuries past, judgments and tribunals were conducted beneath its shade.

The Linden tree path through life

Linden tree-born people belong to the family of Water elements, the source of their gift for empathy. Their sympathetic natures long to open up and connect with others, to touch people deep within their hearts and to be touched themselves. However, they have a tendency to take on the cares and woes of others and to suffer along with them. It is therefore important that Linden tree-born people also learn to take care of themselves and to set boundaries at the right time. Setting boundaries does not mean

The heart-opening power of honesty

slamming the door in the face of others or hardening their very generous hearts if they are asked for help. It is more a case of recognizing in good time when they have had enough and to be able to say no in a respectful and loving way, and to pay attention to their own needs. If they don't, they will often do more harm to themselves than they do good to others with their help and support.

Known to the Celts as the "tree of justice," the Linden endows those born under it as a birth sign with a highly developed sense of justice and a gift for diplomacy. Inquiries and tribunals were once held under its boughs, as the Linden tree was thought to inspire mercy in those passing judgment and to bring the truth to light. Linden personalities therefore make excellent judges, teachers, or philosophers, who always allow their heart to have the last word. Linden tree-born people are also highly self-critical, which spurs them on to always do their best in private and professional settings. In this respect, they should always take care to ensure a balance between give and take and not to apply their own and often too (self-)critical standards to others. We are all entitled to have our own truths, values, and standards.

The symmetrical shape of the Linden leaf can remind us of this; together, its two halves form a heart, just as Linden tree-born people can see themselves reflected in their polar opposites, helping them to recognize who they really are. In this way, they can find peace within themselves and with the world.

In a nutshell

"Nobody's perfect" is a dictum that Linden tree-born people should take to heart, as their aim is always to create a balance between heart and head. They should learn not to be so judgmental and harsh on themselves and others; the more they open their heart, which can get right to the crux of matters in the way that their sharp minds can't, the easier they will find it to step away from their need to be perfectionist. In doing so they will learn to respect their own needs and those of others and to give from the fullness of their heart.

Healing powers
The blossom, leaves, and bark of the Linden tree all have anti-pyretic, diaphoretic, and antispasmodic properties, and so are mainly used to treat colds and chills.

Birth-tree power
The heart-opening power of honesty.

Inspiration from a Linden tree personality

Few are those who see with their own eyes and feel with their own hearts.

If you want to live a happy life, tie it to a goal.

Albert Einstein
German-American physicist

Olive Tree

September 23, fall equinox

Element family: Earth

Gifts and talents

Wise, profound, multitalented, rational, and demanding; astute, purposeful, and mentally robust; the ability to live in the moment; relaxed, humorous, resilient, patient, helpful, popular, and successful.

Carpe arborem

I acknowledge the sense in accepting life as it is and will give the lightness and joy of life more space in my heart.

Symbolism

The Olive tree, or *Olea* in Latin, is associated with just one day in the year and represents the fall equinox. At this great turning point in the year's cycle, as the beginning of fall is celebrated, day and night are of equal length. It is therefore a day dedicated to balance and harmony. We thank Nature for the harvest that will see us through the approaching winter and pause once again to think in gratitude about the experiences and insights the last few months have brought us before finally letting them go. This ritual helps us to continue on our way, full of trust and confidence and released from whatever may be weighing us down in the past. The Olive tree is highly symbolic and in many cultures represents peace, love, and loyalty; it is also mentioned on many occasions in the Bible.

The Olive tree path through life

Olive tree-born people belong to the family of Earth elements, the source of their resilience and stability, their deep connection with Mother Earth, and their wisdom. They are grounded,

The responsible power of life wisdom

pragmatic people who are deeply rooted in life. For the Celts, both the Olive tree and the Fig tree were symbols of happiness and prosperity. People with this birth-tree are guided by the vision of getting ever closer to ultimate wisdom on their life path with each new day and experience.

Olive tree personalities know intuitively what is important in life. Hence their skill in being able to mediate between people when conflict arises, helping to restore balance and harmony. Whatever career they choose, Olive tree people enjoy serving a community (in which they will almost always play a leading role), and they also generally manage to make the best of circumstances, not only for themselves but for all concerned.

Olive tree-born people are generally robust and astute in their pursuit of success. The only thing they need to bear in mind is to try and live in a way that is close to Nature, gradually replacing their potentially excessive sense of responsibility and tendency to criticize with a lightness of spirit and pure enjoyment of life, whatever form that takes.

In a nutshell

Charismatic people always exert a powerful influence as role models, which always brings responsibility. Before taking on a leadership role, they should learn to be honest about and stand by their true feelings. Just as the Olive tree seeks the warmth of the sun to grow and mature, it also needs the nourishment of the water that lies concealed in the ground, and so Olive-tree born people need to get in touch with their true feelings. Once they allow themselves to do so, they will find wisdom entering their life.

Healing powers

The oil and leaves of the Olive tree have properties that help strengthen the liver, care for the skin, and lower blood pressure.

Birth-tree power

The responsible power of life wisdom.

Inspiration from Olive tree personalities

I am the author of my destiny and I regret nothing.

Romy Schneider
German-French actress

What makes my heart sing?

Robert Betz
German psychologist and author

Beech

December 22, winter solstice (astronomically generally on December 21)

Element family: Air

Gifts and talents

Secretive, intuitive, with infinite persistence and patience; an ability to act resolutely and conscientiously; consistent, responsible, trustworthy, inspiring; a great organizer and leader, with a large knowledge base.

Carpe arborem

I am always in touch with my roots, which give me intuitive strength and the patience to wait until opportunity reveals itself.

Symbolism

Beech marks the winter solstice and the advent of winter, marking the shortest day and longest night of the year. In almost every country of the world a "festival of light" is held around the time of this solstice; in the West, this is Christmas. To our Celtic forebears, the Beech tree was associated with the mystical secrets of life; the Germanic tribes would carve the rune sticks they used to predict the future from Beech wood. The similarity between the words "Beech" and "book" originates in the fact that the first books made in the West were written on strips of Beech bark.

The Beech path through life

Beech-tree born people belong to the family of Air elements, which lies behind their agile minds that are so quick on the uptake and the speed and expedience with which they achieve their goals. They rarely do this alone, however, as they are very social individuals who enjoy working as part of a team and they usually take on the role and responsibilities of group leader.

The enduring power of purpose and focus

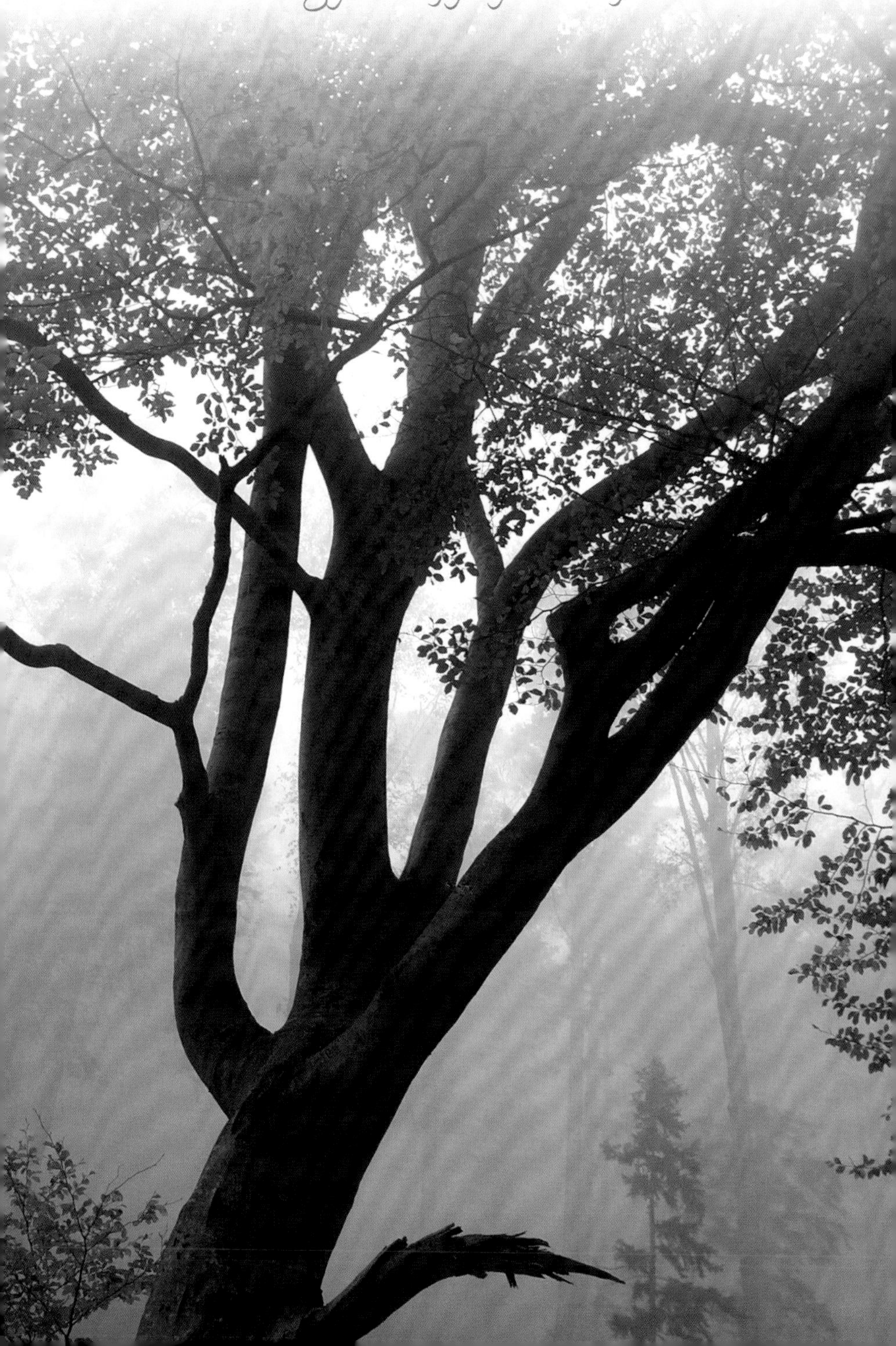

If Beech personalities learn to trust their emotions and their gift for intuition, their decisions will help them to achieve the group's common goal. However, what truly marks out a born leader is not just self-confidence, assertiveness, and a sense of duty, but, importantly, also an ability to be tolerant and to demonstrate empathy, especially toward those people who may be more sensitive by nature.

Beech personalities nonetheless tend to be excessively strict, critical, and intolerant, suggesting an inherent sense of inferiority. This makes it difficult for them to express their feelings in a genuine way. Beech-born people should never lose sight of the fact that the potential of a community—whether among friends and family, or in business or out in the wider world—is based on mutual trust and is a function of the diversity, individuality, and creativity of its different members. The art of being a leader is to recognize and nurture each person's talents and combine them into a whole for the greater success of a project.

In a nutshell

Beech-born people should learn to value themselves more as human beings and not to define themselves merely in terms of their achievements. An important first step here is to be trusting and to learn to accept and give their feelings space, and to be able to express them.

Despite their qualities as leaders, Beech-born people should recognize that arbitrary dominance and the exercise of power over others will only bring them success in the short term; each family member or member of a group should be valued equally. The sense of belonging that this engenders gives everyone courage and strength, powering the group onward toward achieving its goals.

Healing powers
The bark, wood, leaves, and fruits of the Beech have disinfectant, antipyretic, and anti-inflammatory properties.

Birth-tree power
The enduring power of purpose and focus.

Inspiration from a Beech personality

You have to lift up the audience to you, you can't descend to its level.

A worthy foe will take us further than a dozen worthless friends.

Gustaf Gruendgens
German actor and director

JANUARY

1 **Apple tree**
2
3
4
5
6
7
8
9
10
11
12
13
14
15
16
17
18
19
20
21
22
23
24
25
26
27
28
29
30
31

Fir

Elm

Cypress

Famous Fir tree personalities   January 2–11

One's life has value so long as one attributes value to the life of others, by means of love, friendship, indignation, and compassion.
Simone de Beauvoir (French writer, political activist, and feminist)

Greta Thunberg (Swedish environmental activist)
Khalil Gibran (Lebanese-American poet and philosopher)

Famous Elm personalities   January 12–24

Love is the key to the solution of the world's problem, yes, even love for enemies.
Martin Luther King (American civil rights activist)

Kate Moss (British supermodel)
Muhammad Ali (American boxing world champion)

Famous Cypress personalities   January 25–February 3

No matter how big the idea, or how vast the project, everything starts the same way—with one small moment.
Shakira (Columbian singer and songwriter)

Oprah Winfrey (American talk show host)
Wolfgang Amadeus Mozart (Austrian composer)

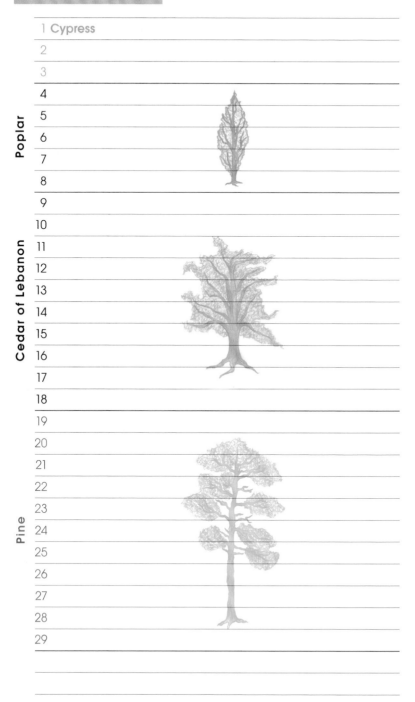

1 Cypress
2
3
4
5
6
7
8
9
10
11
12
13
14
15
16
17
18
19
20
21
22
23
24
25
26
27
28
29

Poplar

Cedar of Lebanon

Pine

Famous Poplar personalities February 4–8

Love the life you live. Live the life you love.

Don´t forget your history nor your destiny.

You never know how strong you are until being strong is the only choice.

Bob Marley (Jamaican singer and songwriter)

Rosa Parks (American activist in the civil rights movement)
James Dean (American actor)

Famous Cedar of Lebanon personalities February 9–18

You cannot teach a man anything, you can only help him find it within himself.

Galileo Galilei (Italian philosopher, astronomer, and physicist).

Mia Farrow (American actress and activist)
Thomas Edison (American inventor)

Famous Pine personalities February 19–29

Change your opinions, keep to your principles; change your leaves, keep intact your roots.

Victor Hugo (French author)

Kristin Davis (American actress)
Steve Jobs (American founder of Apple)

Willow

1
2
3
4
5
6
7
8
9
10

Linden tree

11
12
13
14
15
16
17
18
19
20
21 Oak

Hazel

22
23
24
25
26
27
28
29
30
31

Famous Willow personalities   March 1–10

Peace is to be found only in forests.

Death and love are the two wings that bear the good man to heaven.

Michelangelo (Italian Renaissance sculptor and painter)

Sharon Stone (American actress)
Antonio Vivaldi (Italian composer)

Famous Linden tree personalities   March 11–20

It is the supreme art of the teacher to awaken joy in creative expression and knowledge.

We cannot solve problems by using the same kind of thinking we used when we created them.

Albert Einstein (German physicist and Nobel Prize laureate)

Ruth Bader Ginsburg (American Associate Justice of the Supreme Court of the United States)
Bruce Willis (American actor)

Famous Oak personalities   March 21 (spring equinox)

I am not designed to come second or third. I am designed to win!

Ayrton Senna (Brazilian racing driver)

Kalani Brown (American basketball player)
Joseph Fourier (French mathematician and physicist)

Famous Hazel personalities   March 22–31

Do not quench your inspiration and your imagination; do not become the slave of your model.

Great things are not done by impulse, but by a series of small things brought together.

Vincent van Gogh (Dutch painter)

Lady Gaga (American singer, songwriter and actress)
Elton John (British singer and songwriter)

APRIL

Rowan

1
2
3
4
5
6
7
8
9
10

Maple

11
12
13
14
15
16
17
18
19
20

Walnut

21
22
23
24
25
26
27
28
29
30

Famous Rowan personalities   April 1–10

The advice I would give to someone is to not take anyone's advice.
Eddie Murphy (American actor and comedian)

Wangari Muta Maathai (Kenyan activist and Nobel Peace Prize laureate)

Kristen Stewart (American actress)

Famous Maple personalities   April 11–20

True knowledge always comes from the heart.

Simplicity is the ultimate form of sophistication.
Leonardo da Vinci (Italian polymath)

Emma Watson (British actress)
Charlie Chaplin (British comic actor and filmmaker)

Famous Walnut personalities   April 21–30

For peace to reign on Earth, humans must evolve into new beings who have learned to see the whole first.

One who makes himself a worm cannot complain afterwards if people step on him.
Immanuel Kant (German philosopher)

Jessica Alba (American actress)
Max Planck (German physicist and Nobel Prize laureate)

Yew

1
2
3
4
5
6
7
8
9
10
11
12
13
14
15

Horse chestnut

16
17
18
19
20
21
22
23
24

Ash

25
26
27
28
29
30
31

Famous Yew personalities   May 1–14

There are often some hundred times, a thousand times, before you can really see it for the first time.

Christian Morgenstern (German author)

Jane Jacobs (American-Canadian journalist, author, and activist)
Robert Pattinson (British actor)

Famous Horse chestnut personalities   May 15–24

You can get totally messed up trying to please everyone with what you do, but ultimately, you have to please yourself.

Pierce Brosnan (Irish actor and film producer)

Enya (Irish singer and songwriter)
Grace Jones (Jamaican model, singer and songwriter, record producer, and actress)

Famous Ash personalities   May 25–June 3

It's often just enough to be with someone. I don't need to touch them. Not even talk. A feeling passes between you both. You're not alone.

If I'd observed all the rules, I'd never have got anywhere.

Marilyn Monroe (American actress and model)

Kylie Minogue (Australian singer and songwriter)
John F Kennedy (35th president of the United States)

1 **Ash**

2

3

4

5

6

7

8

9

10

11

12

13

14

15

16

17

18

19

20

21

22

23

24 Birch

25

26

27

28

29

30

Hornbeam

Fig tree

Apple tree

Famous Hornbeam personalities   June 4–13

From one hundred educated and sensitive people, already today ninety would never eat meat again if they had to kill or stab to death the animal that they eat themselves.

Bertha von Suttner (Austrian Nobel Peace Prize laureate)

Anna Kournikova (American-Russian tennis player)
Johnny Depp (American actor)

Famous Fig tree personalities   June 14–23

By helping others, you will learn how to help yourselves.

Aung San Suu Kyi (Burmese politician, freedom fighter, and Nobel Peace Prize laureate)

Lionel Richie (American singer, songwriter, and composer)
Edward Snowden (American whistleblower)

Famous Birch personalities   24 June (Saint John's Day)

A child´s smile is worth more than all the money in the world.

Lionel Messi (Argentine footballer)

Mindy Kaling (American author, actress, and producer)
Jack Dempsey (American boxer)

Famous Apple tree personalities   June 25–July 4

For true love is inexhaustible; the more you give, the more you have, and if you go to draw at the true fountainhead, the more water you draw, the more abundant is its flow.

I am connected only to the person to whom I give a gift. I understand only that person I approach in love. I exist only where the sources of my roots bring me water.

Antoine de Saint-Exupéry (French author)

Diana, Princess of Wales
Franz Kafka (Bohemian novelist and writer)

1 **Apple tree**
2
3
4
5
6
7
8
9
10
11
12
13
14
15
16
17
18
19
20
21
22
23
24
25
26
27
28
29
30
31

Fir

Elm

Cypress

Famous Fir personalities   July 5–14

If you think you are too small to make a difference, try sleeping with a mosquito.

Dalai Lama (Tibetan monk and spiritual leader)

Susan Wojcicki (American businesswoman, CEO of YouTube)
Tom Hanks (American actor)

Famous Elm personalities   July 15–25

Your playing small doesn't serve the world. What counts in life is not the mere fact that we have lived, it is what difference we have made to the lives of others.

Courage is not the absence of fear but the triumph over it. The brave man is not he who does not feel afraid, but he who conquers that fear.

Nelson Mandela (former president of South Africa, Nobel Peace Prize laureate)

Angela Merkel (German politician)
Daniel Radcliffe (British actor)

Famous Cypress personalities   July 26–August 4

Anyone who perceives his shadow and his light simultaneously sees himself from two sides and thus gets in the middle.

Carl Gustav Jung (Swiss psychologist)

JK Rowling (British author)
Barack Obama (44th president of the United States and Nobel Peace Prize laureate)

1 Cypress
2
3
4
5
6
7
8
9
10
11
12
13
14
15
16
17
18
19
20
21
22
23
24
25
26
27
28
29
30
31

Poplar

Cedar of Lebanon

Pine

Famous Poplar personalities   August 5–13

People don't always express their inner thoughts to one another;
a conversation may be quite trivial, but often the eyes will reveal
what a person really thinks or feels.

Alfred Hitchcock (British film director and screenwriter)

Whitney Houston (American singer)
Andy Warhol (American artist, film director, and producer)

Famous Cedar of Lebanon personalities   August 14–23

The most courageous act is still to think for yourself. Aloud.

Coco Chanel (French fashion designer)

Madonna (American singer and actress)
Earvin "Magic" Johnson (American basketball player)

Famous Pine personalities   August 24–September 2

The good you do today may be forgotten tomorrow. Do good any-
way. Give the world the best you have and it may never be enough.
Give your best anyway. For you see, in the end, it is between you
and God. It was never between you and them anyway.

Mother Teresa of Calcutta
(Albanian-Indian Catholic nun and missionary)

Keanu Reeves (Canadian actor)
Michael Jackson (American singer and songwriter)

Willow

1 Pine
2
3
4
5
6
7
8
9
10
11
12
13

Linden tree

14
15
16
17
18
19
20
21
22

Hazel

23 Olive tree
24
25
26
27
28
29
30

My definition of stupid is wasting your opportunity to be yourself, because I think everybody has a uniqueness and everybody´s good at something.

Pink (American singer)

Pippa Middleton (British author and columnist)
Jon Bon Jovi (American singer and songwriter)

Visualization—it's been huge for me. Your mind doesn't know the difference between imagination and reality. You can't always practice perfectly—my fingers will play a little bit out of tune, or my dance moves might not be as sharp—but in my mind, I can practice perfectly.

Lindsey Stirling (American violinist, dancer, and songwriter)

Sophia Loren (Italian actress)
Leonard Cohen (Canadian poet, singer, songwriter, and novelist)

A time comes when you need to stop waiting for the man you want to become and start being the man you want to be.

Bruce Springsteen (American singer and songwriter)

Romy Schneider (German-French actress)
Ray Charles (American singer and musician)

Your task is not to seek for love, but merely to seek and find all the barriers within yourself that you have built against it.

The wound is the place where the light enters you.

There is a voice that doesn't use words. Listen.

Rumi (medieval Persian mystic and poet)

Avril Lavigne (Canadian singer and songwriter)
Ivan Pavlov (Russian physiologist and Nobel Prize laureate)

1 **Hazel**
2
3
4
5
6
7

Rowan

8
9
10
11
12
13
14
15
16
17

Maple

18
19
20
21
22
23
24
25
26
27

Walnut

28
29
30
31

Famous Rowan personalities   October 4–13

Forgiveness is for yourself because it frees you. It lets you out of the prison that you put yourself in.

> **Louise Hay** (American spiritual thinker and founder and publisher of Hay House)

Matt Damon (American actor)
John Lennon (British singer, songwriter, and peace activist)

Famous Maple personalities   October 14–23

This is the precept by which I have lived: Prepare for the worst; expect the best; and take what comes.

> **Hannah Arendt** (German-born American philosopher and political scientist)

Felicity Jones (British actress)
Oscar Wilde (Irish poet and playwright)

Famous Walnut personalities   October 24–November 2

The purpose of art is washing the dust of daily life off our souls.

Every child is an artist. The problem is how to remain an artist once we grow up.

> **Pablo Picasso** (Spanish painter)

Julia Roberts (American actress and producer)
Peter Jackson (New Zealand film director and producer)

1 **Walnut**

2

3

4

5

6

7

8

9

10

11

12

13

14

15

16

17

18

19

20

21

22

23

24

25

26

27

28

29

30

Yew

Horse chestnut

Ash

Famous Yew personalities   November 3–11

Only you and you alone can change your situation. Don´t blame it on anything or anyone.

People will always judge you because they feel dissatisfied with their own life.

Leonardo DiCaprio (American actor and environmentalist)

Adele (British singer and songwriter)
David Guetta (French DJ)

Famous Horse chestnut personalities   November 12–21

The whole world is a great story and we are characters in it.

If people knew what death is, they would no longer be afraid of it.

Michael Ende (German author)

Whoopi Goldberg (American actress and singer)
Chad Kroeger (Canadian singer, songwriter, and producer)

Famous Ash personalities   November 22–December 1

Kindness is the language which the deaf can hear and the blind can see.

Mark Twain (American writer and publisher)

Tina Turner (American singer)
Scarlett Johansson (American actress and singer)

DECEMBER

1 **Ash**

2

3

4

5

6

7

8

9

10

11

12

13

14

15

16

17

18

19

20

21

22 **Beech**

23

24

25

26

27

28

29

30

31

Hornbeam

Fig tree

Apple tree

Famous Hornbeam personalities   December 2–11

Each person comes into this world with a specific destiny—he has something to fulfill, some message has to be delivered, some work has to be completed.

Osho (Indian philosopher)

Emily Dickinson (American poet)
Walt Disney (American film producer and entrepreneur)

Famous Fig tree personalities   December 12–21

Art must once again be a bridge between the creativity of nature and the creativity of man.

If we do not honor our past we lose our future. If we destroy our roots, we cannot grow.

Friedensreich Hundertwasser (Austrian artist)

Christina Aguilera (American singer, songwriter, and actress)
Brad Pitt (American actor)

Famous Beech personalities   December 22 (winter solstice)

Inspiration is an awakening, a quickening of all man's faculties, and it is manifested in all high artistic achievements.

There are many things that I want to tell you – well, really, only one – but that one is as large as the ocean – as the ocean is deep and infinite, so is my love for you and it will be for all my life!

Giacomo Puccini (Italian opera composer)

Vanessa Paradis (French singer, model, and actress)
Maurice Gibb (British singer, songwriter, and producer)

Famous Apple tree personalities   Dec 23–January 1

When I was younger I wish I'd known that what often seemed to be the "end of the world" often turned out to be a positive and transformative experience!

Annie Lennox (British singer and songwriter)

Denzel Washington (American actor and director)
John Legend (American singer, songwriter, and producer)

Acknowledgments

My thanks go to my son Alexander, who taught me the three most important things in life:
- to have courage and face my fears
- to have gratitude for and take joy in the small, often seemingly insignificant gifts that life gives us
- unconditional love

My heartfelt thanks to my family, my friends, and everyone—all the people and creatures who have been my companions during the many and various stages of my life and who have strengthened my belief in my dreams and visions, at once encouraging and reminding me of my path when I lost sight of it amid the tribulations of day-to-day life.

I would like to say a special thank you to Neue Erde Verlag publishers and their team for the editing, design, and printing of this book; I felt I was in good hands right from the start. They have helped to open a new door through which to bring the wisdom of trees out into the world, allowing more people to feel and experience a deep love of Nature once again.

Last but not least, my gratitude is to our forebears, the Celtic people and their Druids. They lived in harmony with Mother Earth, drawing from this bond their strength and their trust in life and themselves; even if much of this has now been forgotten, a part of their wisdom lives on, carefully passed down orally from generation to generation in many old customs. If we can rediscover these customs and bring them into our daily lives, they will show us the way back to our original balance in connection with Nature.

Bibliography and Recommended Reading

These books have been patient teachers and are bursting with facts and information that have accompanied, inspired and enriched me on my path.

Ferrini, Paul: *Love Without Conditions: Reflections of the Christ Mind, Part I*, Heartways Press, 1995

Gibran, Khalil: *The Prophet*, Knopf, 1923

Hageneder, Fred: *The Spirit of Trees: Science, Synthesis and Inspiration*, Floris Books 2000/2017

Kenyon, Tom and Kennedy, Wendy: *Great Human Potential: Walking in One's Own Light—Teaching from The Ninth Dimensional Pleiadians and The Hathors*, Ariane Editions, 2014

Kruta, Venceslas: *The Celts, History and Civilisation*, Hachette Illustrated, 2005

O'Donohue, John: *Anam Cara: A Book of Celtic Wisdom*, Harper Perennial, 1998

Graves, Robert: *The White Goddess: A Historical Grammar of Poetic Myth* (FSG Classics), MacMillan USA, 2013

Vescoli, Michael: *The Celtic Tree Calendar: Your Tree Sign and You*, Souvenir Press, 1999

About the Author

Daniela Christine Huber was born in 1983 and grew up with her grandparents on a remote farm in Austria, where she developed her love for the natural world, and trees in particular, at a very early age.

After taking a degree in biochemistry and gene technology, she worked for an international corporation for several years before starting a course in fine art. She now works as an art teacher and freelance artist, and gives seminars and individual consultations imparting the wisdom of trees to her clients. She lives with her husband and son in a small town in the heart of Austria between Graz and Vienna.

Daniela Christine Huber offers individual consultations of different kinds, including:

- Family birth-tree networks: unconscious beliefs and thought patterns within the family are revealed. This helps to create an awareness of the individuality and the different emotional needs of each family member, creating a unifying perspective on the way family relationships interconnect.
- Workplace birth-tree networks: strengthening and promoting balance and understanding, as well as a healthy and harmonious climate in the workplace.

Check out her website for more information:

www.birth-tree.com

In this full-color guide, the authors explain how to calculate your personal numbers and work with the healing energies of gemstones to unfold the full potential that your numbers reveal. The authors describe which crystals resonate most with each number's energy and offer affirmations, meditations, and crystal healing techniques to connect with gemstone energies.

Editha Wuest, Sabine Schieferle
Crystals and Numerology
Decode Your Numbers and
Support Your Life Path with Healing Stones
Paperback, full-color throughout, 160 pages
ISBN 978-1-64411-273-1

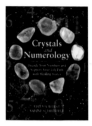

There are two types of angels: those with wings, and those with leaves. For thousands of years, people seeking advice or wanting to give thanks to Nature have walked the ancient paths into the sacred grove. Since today sacred groves have become rare, and venerable old trees in peaceful surroundings cannot always be found quickly when we need them, we are pleased to offer this oracle deck that can bring us closer to the tree angels once more.

Fred Hageneder
The Tree Angel Oracle Deck
The Ancient Path into the Sacred Grove
Includes 144-page book and 36 full-color cards
ISBN 978-1-64411-038-6

www.earthdancerbooks.com

Music for trees: Celtic harp solo, in dialogue with flute, violin, saxophone, sarod or flugelhorn, with arrangements for string quartet or percussion.

Fred Hageneder
The Spirit of Trees
CD, 66 minutes,
8-page booklet
EAN 5016700132021

Fred Hageneder
The Silence of Trees
CD, 72 minutes, 8-page booklet
EAN 5016700132120

Audio samples at
www.earthheartmusic.com

Huna is an ancient shamanic tradition from Hawaii that recognizes seven elemental Nature powers into which we can tap anywhere and at any time. Connect your soul with water, fire, wind, rock, plants, animals, and beings of light. The easy-to-implement exercises, techniques, and rituals presented in this book will enable you to draw on the strength of the natural forces for empowerment.

Susanne Weikl
The Seven Elemental Forces of Huna
Practices for Tapping into the Energies of Nature
from the Hawaiian Tradition
Paperback, full-color throughout, 128 pages
ISBN 978-1-62055-885-0

In this full-color pocket guide featuring beautiful animal photos, the authors introduce 45 important spirit animals alphabetically and explore their wisdom. They provide a meditative journey to help you discover which animal is your personal soul companion and offer practices to intuitively find the right power animal for a given situation.

Phillip Kansa, Elke Kirchner-Young
Animal Spirit Wisdom
A Pocket Reference to 45 Power Animals
Paperback, full-color throughout, 112 pages
ISBN 978-1-64411-115-4

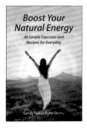

This handy pocket guide presents 40 easy, quick, yet effective ways to boost your energy, rebuild your focus, enhance performance, get better sleep, and bring your life back into balance. It includes simple mental and physical techniques, several recipes, as well as an index of the methods ordered by desired effect.

Sandy Taikyu Kuhn Shimu
Boost Your Natural Energy
40 Simple Exercises and Recipes for Everyday
Paperback, full-color throughout, 96 pages
978-1-62055-974-1

For further information and to request a book catalog contact:
Inner Traditions, One Park Street, Rochester, Vermont 05767

Earthdancer Books is an Inner Traditions imprint.
Phone: +1-800-246-8648, customerservice@innertraditions.com
www.earthdancerbooks.com • www.innertraditions.com

AN INNER TRADITIONS IMPRINT